Contents

D0887298

FOREWORD iii

ACKNOWLEDGMENTS v

THE BASICS 1
   Commercial diplomacy and the national interest 1
   The rise of commercial diplomacy 5
   Organization 7
   Embassies and ambassadors 9
   Resources 10
   Who gets help 12

BUILDING A STRATEGY 16
   Open communications 17
   Weapons and defense 25
   Long-term planning 29

MARKET ACCESS 38
   High-level attention 39
   Private sector action 43
   Creating markets 51
   Commercial aviation 53
   Investment access 56
   Complex barriers, patient persuasion 59
   Starting from scratch 64

RULES 69
   Property 70
   Bribery 86
   Contracts 96

SECURITY 106
   Sanctions and export controls 106
   Securing the borders 110

CONCLUSION 118
   Recommendations 120

APPENDICES 122
NOTES 125
INDEX 131

Foreword

This thoughtful book, *Commercial Diplomacy and the National Interest*, dramatizes the importance of commercial advocacy to the United States. Through stories and case histories, Harry Kopp articulates the close relationship between trade, investment and other commercial activities and broader national interests.

Commercial advocacy has not always been one of our country's highest diplomatic priorities. For many years, our senior policy makers and diplomats did not fully recognize the critical importance of commerce. Many senior foreign policy officers saw the development of trade and investment as the responsibility of the Commerce Department, the Export-Import Bank and other agencies, but not one of the highest priorities of the Department of State or the National Security Council. It's difficult to determine when commercial diplomacy became one of the nation's highest foreign policy priorities. Kopp, a former foreign service officer himself, suggests that former Secretary of State Larry Eagleburger's 1989 proclamation of a "Bill of Rights for Business" marked the moment when the State Department and other U.S. senior policy makers put trade and investment at the top of the country's agenda.

Secretary Eagleburger was a passionate advocate for this change in U.S. policy priorities. Because of my previous experience in the Commerce Department where I had been an assistant secretary of Trade Development and undersecretary before I became President George H.W. Bush's ambassador to Iceland, Secretary Eagleburger encouraged me to create two awards in the State Department for commercial advocacy—one that honors a career ambassador and a second that rewards a career foreign service officer who is not an ambassador. The undersecretary of state for economic affairs chairs the Cobb Award selection committee, which includes a member of Congress (usually the chairman of the Senate Foreign Relations Committee or the House International Relations Committee), prominent international business leaders and other senior government officials. This prestigious committee has given the Cobb Award a high profile within the State Department. The competition for the award among our country's most dynamic ambassadors and other foreign service officers promotes innovation in commercial advocacy and ensures that the best ideas and techniques are recognized and publicized throughout the foreign service.

In that same spirit, this book shows diplomats and business leaders the many different ways they can and must work together to their mutual benefit. Students and practitioners of foreign policy and international business who read this book will come away with a better understanding of the strategic importance of international commerce to overall U.S. interests.

Charles E. Cobb, Jr.
May 2004

Acknowledgments

The Business Council for International Understanding and the American Academy of Diplomacy gratefully acknowledge the support of the Nelson B. Delavan and Una Chapman Cox Foundations, and the support of Ambassador Charles E. Cobb, Jr. Without their help this publication would not have been possible.

The author thanks the many corporations and individuals whose cooperation made it possible to tell their stories in this book. Any errors are the responsibility of the author alone.

The author is also grateful to Ambassadors Charles A. Gillespie, William C. Harrop, Robert V. Keeley, L. Bruce Laingen and Langhorne A. Motley, and to Riva Levinson, George Pickart, Peter Tichansky and Vicki Weil for their assistance and editorial advice. Bradley Steiner, Jr. of the American Academy of Diplomacy and Jacqueline Corr of the Business Council for International Understanding provided strong staff support. Cover design and manuscript layout are the work of Helen Glenn Court, who also edited the final text.

The Basics

Security and prosperity are the two great goals of American foreign policy, and they are closely linked. The United States, with less than 5 percent of the world's population, produces 32 percent of the world's goods and services. It is the world's leading exporter, the world's leading importer, and the world's primary source and destination of funds for foreign investment. Our position as the best place in the world to do business—the most reliable in which to buy, the most lucrative in which to sell, and the safest and surest in which to invest or to raise capital—is a cause, not an effect, of American global leadership.

Our prosperity and openness are a magnet to the world, as immigration patterns over more than a century attest. Other countries strive for what we have achieved. They want to know how we got where we are, and whether our methods can be adapted to their circumstances. Our economic power is essential to our strength. More than our military power or cultural prominence, our economic and commercial strength and global presence are the source of our leadership in world affairs, because they are the source of the willingness of others to follow.

Commercial diplomacy involves business and government overseas in cooperative efforts to achieve commercial objectives that advance national interests. Successful commercial diplomacy adds to America's economic power.

In the pages that follow, we will see how commercial diplomacy works. We will look at stories and case histories from the fiercely competitive world of international business, at challenges posed, strategies adopted, tactics executed and results achieved. There are winners and losers, deals sealed and deals blown, money and jobs made and lost. It's a lively and important tale.

Commercial diplomacy and the national interest

For more than fifty years, whatever the swings in business and political cycles, American commercial policy and American commercial diplomacy have sought to expand international trade and investment.

Global growth and economic development depend on our success. Trade leads growth: world trade has grown faster than world output in forty of the past fifty years. Over that period, trade is up about 1,900 percent, output about 650 percent and population about 240 percent.

Foreign direct investment sends technology and entrepreneurship around the world, lifting productivity, wages and standards of living. Over the past thirty years, around the world, direct investment coming from abroad has grown three times faster than direct investment from domestic sources. Global inflows of foreign direct investment rose from under $13 billion in 1970 to $1.5 trillion in 2000 before falling back to $800 billion in 2002.

This worldwide expansion of trade and investment is evidence of the globalization of economic activity. Globalization—the rationalization of production, trade and investment on a global scale—is driven by rapid advances in communications and information technology. But it is built on the sturdy political framework of international economic cooperation developed after World War II and strengthened by fifty years of nearly continuous multilateral negotiation.

The World Trade Organization, the International Monetary Fund and the World Bank have expanded their membership toward universality as well as the breadth and depth of the rights and obligations that the membership entails. Without these cooperative structures, technological change would produce different and less beneficial results, and there would be no rules or principles to constrain companies or governments in their competition for markets.

The expansion of global commerce and the negotiated structure that supports it are vital elements in American and international security. International commercial relationships supplement, reinforce and lend substance and stability to relations between governments. Political relationships can turn in an instant from warm to cool, from friendly to hostile. Business relationships tend to be steadier. An aircraft sale, for example, may be signed in a day, but finance, delivery, training and maintenance may last for ten or twenty years. An international oil or gas pipeline creates linkages that endure for many decades.

It's an old truth of international affairs that when goods and services cross borders, armies don't. Tom Friedman of the *New York Times* made the same point when he observed that no two countries with a McDonald's have ever gone to war. It is no coincidence that the most dangerous areas of the world are the least engaged in the global economic system. The WTO has 147 members. Afghanistan, Iran, Iraq, Lebanon, Libya, North Korea and Syria are not among them.

Because international commerce so clearly serves national and public interests, businesses that seek to place their goods, services or capital abroad deserve the support of their government. Most governments around the world are quick to provide it. Most presidents and prime ministers, as well as the occasional king, prince and potentate, are eager salesmen, ready to bring to bear such leverage as they can muster to win one for the home team.

In the United States, though, government and business are more standoffish. The public is skeptical of business motives: has anyone ever seen a movie in which a corporation was the good guy? Public wariness makes some officials leery of too close an identification with commercial interests. And business executives are sometimes timid about asking for official support, lest they be accused of buying favors or soaking up corporate welfare.

The sense that global business and the national interest are at odds should not persist. The United States is the world's largest exporter. Merchandise exports in 2003 were $714 billion, supporting nearly sixteen million high-paying jobs.[1] The United States is also the world's largest importer, with merchandise imports reaching $1.3 billion in 2003. Total U.S. imports and exports of goods and services were over $2.5 trillion in 2003, about 23 percent of gross domestic product and about 15 percent of all world trade.[2]

The United States is the world's largest source and destination of foreign direct investment as well. At the end of 2002, American direct investments abroad totaled over $1.5 trillion, and foreigners had made direct investments of over $1.3 trillion in the United States.[3] Foreign investments, direct and indirect, finance the U.S. trade deficit. In 2003, foreign investment in the United States was $857 billion, of which $86 billion was direct investment. U.S. investment abroad was $278 billion. The difference was a net financial inflow of $579 billion, more than sufficient to cover the U.S. trade deficit ($549 billion on goods, $490 billion on goods and services, $542 billion on current account).[4]

Recently American foreign direct investment abroad has come under political attack. Some have suggested that when American companies invest abroad, they export jobs instead of goods and services and thereby undermine American prosperity. Extensive research on this topic over the past thirty years has failed to support this thesis,[5] and the growing domestic prosperity that has accompanied the globalization of American business surely disproves it.

The argument over foreign investment is hardly new. Over thirty years ago, after a long debate that closely resembles today's fight over outsourcing and "exporting America," Congress rejected a bill that would have placed severe restrictions on outward investment.[6] Since that 1971 decision, the United States has been the world's leading supplier of foreign direct investment, and the average American's income, adjusted for inflation, has risen from $18,800 to over $36,000 per year.[7]

Over this period, the United States has also been the world's leading recipient of foreign direct investment. Are foreign companies hollowing out their own economies by exporting jobs to America? Are they chasing our high-priced labor or our tough environmental standards? Probably not. More likely they understand what American firms also know, that it pays to be close to your major markets. They understand as well that the business climate in the United States is excellent. We have an educated and extremely productive work force. Innovation is welcomed. Rules are transparent, stable and enforced, capital markets are deep and responsive, and borders are open. These are assets we need to protect to remain competitive.

The spread of American ideas about markets and laws, including property rights, contracts and settlement of disputes, depends on American economic primacy. It is no stretch to say that U.S. global economic leadership is essential to the spread of the idea of the rule of law itself. If the United States loses its attraction as a place to do business, or if American companies lose their reputation as good people with whom to do business, American leadership in all fields will suffer. The United States must protect its commercial standing.

Advancing this interest requires cooperation and trust between government and business. In multilateral negotiations, government and business need to work closely together to make sure that global rules are broadly helpful, understood the same way everywhere, enforceable and enforced. In business deals, companies need to be able to count on U.S. embassies abroad and government agencies at home for sound advice on local conditions and strong support against trade barriers and discriminatory treatment. Government needs to provide every possible assistance to make sure that the honest, open practices of American enterprise are sources of strength, not handicaps, in international competition. And Washington needs to make sure that the constraints of security, particularly in policing the flow of people and products across the U.S. border, do not isolate American business from its customers and suppliers.

These challenges to commercial diplomacy are no less difficult for being clear. Are we up to the task?

The rise of commercial diplomacy

For a long time after World War II, the United States could afford to ignore commercial diplomacy, at least with regard to export promotion. Well into the 1960s, Washington's ability to sell abroad was limited only by the ability of customers to pay. Until Europe and Japan recovered—with American economic support—American industry and agriculture had little competition. And trade was simply not a very important factor in the American economy. As late as 1970, exports and imports of goods and services together came to just 10.7 percent of gross domestic product, among the lowest ratios in the world.

But that picture soon changed, dramatically. The Arab oil embargo of 1973 and the oil price shocks of 1973 and 1979 got America's attention. As import bills rose, so did the drive to export. By 1980, the dollar value of U.S. exports and imports of goods and services was five times what it had been at the beginning of the decade. As a share of the economy, foreign trade had grown to 20.2 percent.

The administration and the Congress discovered commercial diplomacy. Protection and promotion of U.S. commercial interests took on a level of priority previously reserved for matters of national security. Legislation enacted in 1980 created the Foreign Commercial Service (FCS), later renamed the U.S. and Foreign Commercial Service, in the Department of Commerce. The authority and responsibilities of the U.S. Trade Representative's Office were greatly expanded. Ambassadors were instructed that "each chief of mission to a foreign country shall have as a principal duty the promotion of U.S. goods and services for export."[8] In plainer language, ambassadors were told to fly the commercial flag and keep commercial interests at the front of their concerns.

The organizational changes posed some challenges for the Department of State. As the Commerce Department added personnel overseas to staff the FCS, the State Department had to reduce its overseas staff by an equal number. But the State Department's leadership was determined to strengthen commercial diplomacy at every level. Commercial responsibilities were added to the portfolios of the economic undersecretary and assistant secretary. The department established a new office of commercial and business affairs to be an "American desk," a strong advocate within the department for U.S. commercial interests. With the help of the Business Council for International Understanding, a sponsor of this book, the department revamped its training courses to give more time and emphasis to commercial affairs.

Personnel evaluations were redesigned to reward demonstrated skill in commercial diplomacy. Ambassadors and foreign service officers who excelled in promoting U.S. commercial interests were recognized through a new awards program, named for the program's benefactor, Ambassador Charles Cobb. And, most dramatically, Deputy Secretary of State Larry Eagleburger proclaimed a "Bill of Rights for American Business." That document, reproduced at Appendix I, is still in force and remains a guide and standard for commercial work across the U.S. government.

In the years since the "Bill of Rights," commercial diplomacy has continued to grow in importance. Ambassador Cobb says "there has been a sea change in the attitude" of senior officials toward commercial advocacy, trade, investment and economic relations. Ambassador John Wolf, one of America's most experienced and distinguished diplomatic professionals,[9] adds, "I have not met a U.S. ambassador appointed in the past two decades who does not believe that economic and commercial issues are high priorities."

The rise of commercial diplomacy is not a partisan phenomenon. The first Bush administration developed and promulgated "Advocacy Guidelines" to help government and business sort out the situations in which official support for a company's overseas efforts would be appropriate, and at what level. The Clinton administration created the Advocacy Center, a unit in the Department of Commerce that implements those guidelines and coordinates the work of the many U.S. agencies involved in commercial promotion. At the Department of State, two of the strongest champions of commercial work have been Joan Spero, appointed by President Clinton as undersecretary for economic, business and agricultural affairs, and Alan Larson, a career foreign-service officer who has served in that same post under both President Clinton and President George W. Bush. At the Department of Commerce, Secretary Ron Brown and Undersecretary Jeffrey Garten in the Clinton administration were extraordinarily energetic and successful advocates for American business interests overseas; Secretary Don Evans and Undersecretary Grant Aldonas follow their leads today.

John Wolf notes, however, that the work of commercial diplomacy does not always receive the professional recognition that it deserves. In the Department of State, Wolf sees "a mental institutional division between economic policy and national security policy" that treats economic affairs as separate and not quite equal. In his own experience, however, Wolf says "security and economics are irrevocably intertwined."

Wolf cites three examples. In Malaysia, where he served as ambassador, he persuaded the U.S. aerospace industry to return to a contest it had abandoned to sell fighter aircraft to the Malaysian air force. With the embassy's full backing, the United States won the sale (and Wolf won the Cobb Award). "The sale not only generated profits for a U.S. company and its partners," Wolf writes, but it also created high-paying jobs for American workers and contributed tangibly to our security goals in East Asia. We wanted to ensure that regional armed forces procured equipment that could function smoothly with our own in joint operations."

Later, as special adviser to the president and the secretary of state for Caspian Basin energy diplomacy, Wolf sought to promote a secure pipeline across the Caucasus that would give Western buyers secure access to Caspian and Central Asian oil. "American firms were prepared to make enormous capital commitments to develop Caspian Basin reserves," Wolf writes. "As a government official, I was asking them to make U.S. and regional political interests a part of their risk-reward calculation. They, in return, were asking me to persuade the heads of state of newly emerging democracies and long-standing U.S. allies to set up a framework that sheltered them from political and legal risk."

And in his current position as assistant secretary of state for non-proliferation affairs, Wolf writes that "building coalitions of like-minded business and government leaders" is "essential to preventing the spread of dangerous technology" from the former Soviet Union. "Dozens of U.S. business partners" are finding new uses for former Soviet weapons laboratories, using "their scientists' expertise for new commercial research and development in a variety of civilian applications, including vaccine development, animal husbandry and microelectronics."

This book provides many more examples of the links between commercial diplomacy and the national interest. As Wolf says, commercial diplomacy and security policy are like the "two wheels of a bicycle," in which neither plays the lesser role and both are needed to move forward. Nevertheless, he says, in the Department of State there is still "an institutional tendency to treat [economic and commercial] issues as distinct from strategic and security concerns." And U.S. companies, he adds, "have had to learn that U.S. embassies can be invaluable business partners."

Organization

Commercial diplomacy is practiced at two levels. One—call it the macro level—involves the negotiation of principles and rules that guide global trade and investment without reference to specific companies, deals or projects. Another—call it the micro or transactional level—involves the contest for sales and contracts and for enforcement in particular cases of prior agreements. The line that separates this macro- and micro-diplomacy is easily crossed. General rules are sometimes proposed with a particular transaction in mind, and individual transactions may be structured to create a precedent. Even so, the distinction is helpful in understanding how the U.S. government develops and conducts commercial diplomacy, and how the agencies involved relate to each other.

At the transactional level where the business gets done, the lead agency varies according to the type of transaction. The most important trade-promotion agency is the Department of Commerce, and in particular the U.S. Commercial Service and the Advocacy Center, especially when small to mid-size business is involved. The Department of Agriculture, and in particular the Foreign Agricultural Service, deals with trade in agricultural commodities and many food products. The Departments of State and Defense usually have the lead in transactions involving weapons systems.

Many agencies beyond these lead agencies have a hand in commercial diplomacy. Indeed, the large number of agencies involved makes formulating and conducting policy unwieldy at best and paralytic at worst. Congress in the 1992 Omnibus Trade Act mandated the creation of a Trade Promotion Coordinating Committee, which the president established in a 1993 executive order that named nineteen agencies as members:[10]

- Department of Commerce (chair)
- Department of State
- Department of the Treasury
- Department of Agriculture
- Department of Energy
- Department of Transportation
- Department of Defense
- Department of Labor
- Department of the Interior
- Agency for International Development
- Trade and Development Agency
- Environmental Protection Agency
- U.S. Information Agency
- Small Business Administration
- Overseas Private Investment Corporation
- Export-Import Bank of the United States

- Office of the U.S. Trade Representative
- Council of Economic Advisers
- Office of Management and Budget
- National Economic Council
- National Security Council.

The Trade Promotion Coordinating Committee (Tpcc) was intended to reduce friction among the agencies, enhance coordination, reduce duplication of effort and develop a "strategic plan" for the government's efforts in export promotion and export finance. But as most observers of the federal government will agree, attempts to resolve interagency conflicts or duplication through reorganization and procedure have not, in general, had lasting success. According to several Tpcc participants, the committee's results fall well short of its goals.

At the macro level, the lead agency is generally the Office of the U.S. Trade Representative, established in 1962 to coordinate trade policy and negotiate trade agreements.[11] The USTR is unique in several ways. It is the only executive-branch agency that by law is responsible to the Congress as well as to the president. And though it is a cabinet-level, operational agency with more than 200 full-time positions in the United States and abroad (at the U.S. missions to the World Trade Organization in Geneva and the European Union in Brussels), it is located within the Executive Office of the President.

Despite USTR's authority, other agencies may lead negotiations on certain issues like trade embargos (State), export controls (Commerce, State and Defense), export credits (Treasury), measures to combat bioterrorism (Homeland Security) and so forth. USTR tries to build policy consensus by chairing a hierarchical structure of cabinet and subcabinet trade policy committees that include the Departments of State, Commerce, Treasury, Agriculture, Labor and others, but interagency friction is imperfectly contained.[12]

Organizational problems largely disappear, however, when an issue is taken out of Washington and placed in a U.S. embassy abroad. In an embassy, the authority of the American ambassador to direct commercial diplomacy is clear.

Embassies and ambassadors

U.S. law provides that a chief of mission "shall have full responsibility" under the president "for the direction, coordination and supervi-

ıf all government executive-branch employees" in his or her country, except for employees under the command of a U.S. area military commander (that is, a geographic combatant commander), or employees assigned to the staff of an international organization. That same law instructs that "each chief of mission to a foreign country shall have as a principal duty the promotion of U.S. goods and services for export to such country."[13]

Every president since John F. Kennedy has reinforced the authority of the ambassador with a letter provided to every chief of mission in a post abroad. The letter from President George W. Bush repeats the language of the law and emphasizes that "you are in charge of all United States government executive branch activities and operations." The president's letter also instructs the chief of mission to "report to me through the secretary of state."[14]

When an ambassador exercises his authority and provides clear leadership, interagency rivalry is suppressed. The directors general of the State Department's foreign service and Commerce Department's commercial service agreed that overseas there is little tension between their agencies, or between their agencies and the many other government bodies that may be involved in any particular case. "An ambassador has flexibility to match the skills of the officer to the demands of the task, without worrying too much about the name of the officer's home agency," said Commerce's Carlos Poza, "and he or she should do so."

The vigorous exercise of the ambassador's authority to direct the activities of all agency representatives in his country may also allow an embassy to mediate disputes that arise in Washington. "The embassy serves as a link between the policy level and the commercial level," said Ambassador Bob Pearson, director general of the foreign service. "The embassy feeds commercial realities into the policy process." The embassy can integrate business necessities, political issues and macro-economics in a way that Washington agencies, each with its own perspective, find difficult to do.

Resources

Ambassadors hold the key to the success of America's commercial diplomacy, but they do not always recognize its importance at home. There has been some improvement in recent years, but congressional staff on the committees that control appropriations for State and Commerce say that ambassadors often fail to appreciate the extent to which successful commercial diplomacy can persuade Congress to unlock the resources needed to support the full range of an embassy's activities and a robust and secure American presence overseas.

State Department officials often say their work is underfunded, because—unlike Agriculture's farmers, Commerce's businessmen or Treasury's financial community—State has no constituency that votes. There is some truth to this tale of woe, of course. In the president's fiscal year 2005 budget request, the total foreign affairs budget, summarized in Appendix II, was $31.5 billion, about 7.1 percent of requested discretionary nondefense spending or 1.6 percent of the total budget of $2.0 trillion. Of the $31.5 billion for foreign affairs, the discretionary request for State, Commerce and related agencies was just under $9 billion, including $4.3 billion slated for ongoing diplomatic and consular operations.[15] Senate Appropriations Committee Staff Director Jim Morhard says, "Secretary Powell will get most of what he asks for" because of his stature, but Congress often denied his predecessors and may deny his successors.

The commercial service of the Department of Commerce is budgeted at about $200 million. The budget supports 650 positions, including 250 authorized positions overseas. The State Department has no budget line for commercial work but reported to the Trade Promotion Coordinating Committee that outlays on economic and trade affairs and business services will be about $155 million in fiscal year 2004.

The State Department may undervalue the work it does that has direct impact on the livelihoods and pocketbooks of millions of Americans. Peter Yeo of the House International Relations Committee staff explains: "Ambassadors who come to members for briefings almost never say, 'Do you have companies in your district that we can help?'" Many members of Congress don't know that American embassies play a critical, job-creating role by protecting U.S. companies against corrupt demands or corrupt competitors, negotiating payment of defaulted foreign bonds and other debts, sorting out commercial disputes, issuing visas for business contacts and trainees and the like.

Jim Morhard says the reputation of the Foreign Service for effective performance of commercial diplomacy has improved dramatically in the past seven years. The record is uneven, he adds, because performance depends on leadership, and leadership varies from embassy to embassy abroad and from bureau to bureau in Washington. But the trend is strongly positive.

Would the department have a generally easier time on Capitol Hill if ambassadors and other senior officials worked harder to inform Congress about commercial diplomacy, especially at the transactional level? Maybe so. As this book will show, ambassadors and embassies often make the decisive difference for U.S. firms operating overseas. Yet commercial work can get lost in the rough-and-tumble of high politics. Morhard and Yeo say that without some kind of crisis or scandal, commercial diplomacy is too small a part of either the Foreign Affairs budget line or the appropriations bill for the departments of State, Commerce and Justice to attract sustained congressional attention. But they agree that ambassadors could improve their relations with many individual members by making the connections between their work abroad and the district at home. That kind of connection, they say, can win some critical support at the margin, where close issues are often decided.

Who gets help

Official action to support U.S. goods, services and business interests overseas is part of U.S. law, implemented through various executive orders and agency directives. But the laws do not define, and regulations rarely address, how far official support extends, and who and what precisely should receive it.

There are guidelines, to be sure, administered largely by the Commerce Department's Advocacy Center.[16] The Advocacy Center's basic standard for determining "the nature and extent" of official support in any situation is "the U.S. national interest." More helpfully, the guidelines offer ways to decide when a product or service or company should receive government backing. U.S. content is one: An export receives support if 50 percent of the content, including materials, equipment and labor, is "made in USA." Evenhandedness is another: When two or more U.S. firms are competing against each other, government agencies are not to take sides between them but may argue generically for U.S. goods and services.

But in recent years, the globalization of production, trade and finance have made the determination of national interest and corporate nationality more and more complex. Responses have necessarily become more flexible.

- In one famous case, a foreign company competing against a U.S. company for a third-country contract tried to get the U.S. government out of the game by bringing in a U.S. partner that had an option to participate but no real equity in the deal. The Commerce Department decided that in this case the neutrality rule need not apply. Similar decisions have been made where one bidder's U.S. content, broadly defined, far exceeds another's.

- The 50-percent U.S. content rule now defines "content" to include design, advertising and other support costs. And when a U.S. firm is part of an international consortium bidding on a project, the Commerce Department's Advocacy Center may issue a national-interest determination that allows embassies to provide support, even if the U.S. participation is relatively small.

- A company incorporated and based outside the United States may be treated like an American company if it is beneficially owned by U.S. citizens.

Jay Brandes, the Commerce Department official who developed the analytic procedures for the Commerce Department's Advocacy Center in the early 1990s, points out that these issues arise especially in investment projects and consortium bidding, where there may not be a lot of obvious U.S. content. "You have to look at the impact on employment, repatriation of profits, follow-on sales, transfers of technology and the like," he says. The center's analysis is based on information supplied by the company seeking support, plus input from embassies and other U.S. government agencies.

Rules and guidelines can never provide a manual of instruction for managing all the blurry situations that international competition presents, but the questions of corporate nationality and U.S. interest can in fact easily be made to look more difficult than they really are. "It's not rocket science, it's common sense," Jay Brandes says, adding that many decisions are made at political levels. Ambassadors and other policy officials will rarely go wrong if they rely on good data and good judgment. For example:

What company could be more American than Boeing? What company could be more foreign than its archrival Airbus? Yet Boeing and Airbus have both gone to great lengths to spread their production around the world, partly for economic and partly for political reasons. And both are eager to advertise their global engagement. Boeing says in its annual report: "We are transforming from a company that knows how to market in countries around the world to one that is a 'citizen' of those countries.... We are reaching out globally to find the best talent and technologies.... And we are investing in new facilities throughout the world."[17] Airbus boasts that in 2002 "business placed by Airbus with contractors in the United States reached $5.5 billion, supporting an estimated 120,000 American jobs and hundreds of companies coast-to-coast. Airbus spends more money with suppliers in the United States than in any other country."[18]

So the question looks tricky. But it is not. Global boasting aside, Boeing is clearly American. Depending on the model, about 70 to 85 percent of the value of Boeing's commercial aircraft, excluding the engine, is of U.S. origin. Even if the Airbus "American jobs" figure is taken at face value, Airbus is not close to Boeing, which directly employs 157,000 people in the United States (December 2003) and provides work for some multiple of that figure through its subcontractors. Boeing exports more from the United States than any other company. As a supplier to the Department of Defense, it is an essential part of American's national security.

But Boeing (and Airbus) aircraft may use engines from General Electric or Rolls-Royce. Are GE engines built in France or China more American than Rolls-Royce engines made in England? Are they more American than Rolls-Royce engines built in Indianapolis? Or should the U.S. government line up behind U.S.-owned Pratt & Whitney, which builds its engines in Canada? Should the foreign content of a Boeing aircraft, or the U.S. content of an Airbus, alter the degree to which the U.S. government marshals its resources and spends its political capital to influence a purchasing decision by a foreign buyer? These are tough questions.

The locus of production is important, of course, but so is the ownership and headquarters of the corporation that earns the revenue from a transaction. As General Electric's Mike Gadbaw points out, "[worldwide] revenue solves lots of problems," giving management options for growth that simply don't exist when sales are down. Making a judgment about who to support in our hypothetical engine case takes careful analysis and plenty of consultation. Even then, the issue could end up in the "too hard" box.

Or take another case. Competing consortia of energy companies are bidding to build an oil pipeline. One, with financing through a European syndicate, includes an American company with a 10-percent interest. The other includes no American equity participant but is financed by a group led by New York investment banks. Should Washington back one consortium over the other?

Sometimes an embassy that tries to stay neutral between competing American companies gets caught when one firm is far more assiduous and shows up far more often than the other. In such a case, said one ambassador who dealt with this situation, the embassy should service the company that asks for advice. "The embassy isn't being inequitable, it's just one firm out-competing another."

What if a project is strategically important? When Bob Pearson was U.S. ambassador to Turkey, he committed his embassy fully to support construction of a pipeline to bring oil from the Caspian Sea across Azerbaijan and Georgia to a terminus at the Turkish Mediterranean port of Ceyhan. A Baku-Tbilisi-Ceyhan pipeline, security analysts said, would provide both revenue and a critical element of stability for the weak and poorly governed post-Soviet states of the southern Caucasus, as well as a Western outlet for Caspian and Central Asian hydrocarbons that did not depend on transit through Russia or Iran. And unlike existing Russian routes that used a port on the Black Sea, the proposed pipeline would not entail the huge environmental risk of bringing oil by tanker through the Bosporus Straits.

None of these benefits depended on the nationality of the companies involved. The lead stakeholders in the consortium pushing hardest for the $2.8 billion pipeline project were BP (formerly British Petroleum) with 38 percent and SOCAR the state-owned oil company of Azerbaijan, with 25 percent. U.S. participants Unocal and Delta Hess (a joint venture of Amerada Hess and the Saudi firm Delta Oil) held small shares. The Bechtel Corporation of California was not part of the consortium but was contracted by it for construction and engineering.

"Is BP an American company? I decided that they were," said Pearson, "and I gave them full support." He was not being disingenuous. London-based BP, which merged with the U.S. firms Amoco and ARCO in 1998 and 1999, has about half its assets in the United States, and American investors may own most of the company's traded shares. But if BP's proposed pipeline route were through Iran to the Persian Gulf, it would never have won official American backing. In this case, the strategic context of the question about BP's nationality supplied the answer.

Building a strategy

Government-business collaboration to achieve national and commercial objectives is no spur-of-the-moment affair. This chapter looks at strategic planning in three very different situations: competing for a public-utility contract, competing for a weapons sale and cultivating long-term opportunities and relationships with no immediate transaction in evidence.

In all cases, of course, regular contact and exchange of information will sharply improve the prospects for success. Companies that show up in embassy or Washington offices with a plea for help of course will get it, but the best time to deal with trouble is before it begins. Especially overseas, company representatives and embassy officers both benefit when they take the time to understand each other's purposes and points of view, their scope of action and their constraints.

When information is timely and complete, prompt and often modest measures can often head off problems. When information is late in coming or leaves out critical parts of the story, much more dramatic action may be needed, and the chance of success goes down.

The energy industry offers a few examples that are worth closer attention. Following deregulation, a number of U.S. utilities in the late 1980s and early 1990s began a vigorous and unprecedented expansion into international markets. They found plenty of demand in developing countries for American technology, know-how and management skills, as well as rapidly rising demand for electric power. They also found markets that were unfamiliar in many ways, dominated by state agencies, price controlled and heavily politicized. Legal protections in many places were unreliable and subject to political manipulation.

Companies that worked closely with U.S. embassies improved their chances of securing contracts and of avoiding the traps and pitfalls of selling to weak, mercurial or unscrupulous governments. Companies that stayed aloof left themselves more vulnerable to flawed contractual arrangements (particularly regarding price controls) or to reliance on inadequate or untrustworthy partners.

Open communications

Two stories stand out as examples of successful commercial diplomacy built on planning and open channels of communication: CMS in Abu Dhabi and AES in Bangladesh. In Abu Dhabi, the embassy's understanding of the local scene allowed it to guide the company through a process that was unfamiliar to all concerned, the first public tender of its kind in a region long accustomed to closed-door practices. In Bangladesh, the company educated the embassy about the intricacies of its effort to win a similarly unprecedented contact, in this case for the country's first privately owned (not to mention foreign-owned) power-generation facility. The company's patient, thorough and honest efforts allowed the ambassador and his staff to intervene persuasively at crucial moments. Then the embassy, AES and Washington agencies together developed programs to increase understanding of energy economics throughout south Asia, making the region far more receptive to proposals from U.S. power-generation companies.

CMS ENERGY: THE AL TAWEELAH A2 PROJECT

CMS Energy, a Michigan-based energy company with annual revenues of about $6 billion, was intrigued by the opportunities for growth in emerging markets. "Even after due diligence," says David Mengebier, senior vice president for government affairs, "prospects looked good: host governments professed eagerness to receive foreign investment, published bidding rules were fair and transparent, and legal and regulatory regimes appeared supportive." But once the competition for a project was engaged, the picture began to change. "Transparent rules grew cloudy, legal safeguards acquired loopholes, regulations began to mutate and the path to success turned swampy."

Under these circumstances the support that ambassadors and their staffs give American companies—providing advice on the local scene and financing requirements, helping to manage or reverse sudden and negative changes in law, policy or regulation, and weighing in with host-country authorities—can often determine whether an investment succeeds or fails.

Mengebier credits strategic advice from American ambassadors and their staffs with a dramatic impact on the company's efforts to develop and sustain business overseas. Mengebier divides embassy assistance into three categories: developing and coordinating advocacy at the start of a bidding process, setting the content and tone of supporting messages from U.S. policy makers to their foreign counterparts, and gathering

18

intelligence to inform and shape the advocacy process as it unfolds. Planning is essential. Mengebier stresses: "It is a mistake to think that commercial diplomacy means taking a few big swings with the blunt instrument of American power to make foreigners buy from American companies. Effective diplomacy, for commercial or other purposes, is never haphazard."

Here is Mengebier's account of commercial diplomacy in support of U.S. participation in the energy sector on the Persian Gulf.

A GREENFIELD PROJECT

The Al Taweelah A2 power project in Abu Dhabi, one of the United Arab Emirates, was a greenfield project—a plant to be built from the ground up. It was the first project of its kind in the Persian Gulf to have private-sector involvement.

Al Taweelah A2 called for construction of both a 710-megawatt power plant and a desalination facility to process 50 million imperial gallons (60 million U.S. gallons) per day of water. According to the rules, the winning bidder would obtain 40-percent ownership of the project, with the remaining 60 percent to be owned by the Abu Dhabi Water and Electric Authority (ADWEA), a government-owned utility. By the time it went into commercial operation in 2001, the total project value of Al Taweelah A2 was approximately $700 million.

Interest in the project was remarkably strong. A pre-qualification process reduced the number of competing firms to eight, and then to three: a French/Belgian consortium, CMS Energy and another American firm. CMS and the European consortium received identical letters, but the other American competitor an entirely different one. Over time it became clear that ADWEA wanted to keep the other American company around as a fallback in the event that negotiations with the two leading contenders broke down. For the U.S. embassy and the U.S. government, the presence of two American firms in the competition complicated the task of identifying the U.S. national interest and advocating accordingly, but as we will see the embassy played a part in navigating those waters as well.

Ambassador David Litt and his Embassy Abu Dhabi played a vigorous and crucial role in the bidding process. The project was the first international competitive bid for a desalination facility in the Gulf and was widely expected to set a standard for many projects to follow. Ambassador Litt recognized the strategic ramifications. A well-run and transparent bidding process that resulted in the selection of an

American firm would encourage significant American investment and trade in a region that historically had been viewed as more receptive to European interests. American private investment would in turn deepen and lend stability to the relationship between the United States and the United Arab Emirates by creating links beyond oil and geopolitics.

Litt made clear to Washington that securing Al Taweelah A2 for an American company was a national priority, and not just for the direct commercial benefits. His strong guidance had an extraordinary impact on the depth and vigor of the U.S. government's advocacy efforts. Washington agencies, including the Commerce Department's Advocacy Center, the Department of Energy and even the White House, were receptive to the embassy's understanding of the project's long-term implications and picked up on the embassy's enthusiasm.

Developing the strategy

In Abu Dhabi, the embassy worked closely with CMS to craft a message, time its delivery and enlist the most potent messengers. Embassy and company employees together plotted the timing of critical points of the bid process and identified the government decision makers who would be most influential at each of those junctures. The answers were not always obvious. Clearly Sheikh Diab, the chairman of ADWEA, would be perhaps the most important, but beyond Sheikh Diab the complexities of politics and family relationships within the Emirate and at a national level were hard to sort through. The embassy helped CMS determine the likely roles of other political leaders, including the president of the Emirates, the crown prince and even the minister of defense.

Working with the Advocacy Center at the Commerce Department in Washington, the embassy designed a series of U.S. government interventions with the decision makers, coordinated among the U.S. agencies involved and timed to coincide with the sequence of the bid process. These interventions were to be made in person, by phone and by letter, and by increasingly senior officials to underscore the depth of the U.S. interest and to lend the appearance of momentum.

By the end of the process, the interventions that began with the political, economic and commercial officers of the embassy extended upward to the ambassador, and included under secretaries from the Departments of State and Commerce, Energy Secretary Bill Richardson, Commerce Secretary William Daley, senior members of the U.S. Congress and ultimately Vice President Gore.

Developing the message

All these messengers needed a consistent and compelling message, with content and tone tailored to the audience. The diplomats and businessmen put together a comprehensive case for CMS Energy, different parts of which would be emphasized by different officials from the U.S. government, depending on their portfolio and the timing and circumstances of the bid process.

The case for CMS emphasized first and foremost the company's successful record as an operator in other markets. At the time, CMS had operations or advanced development efforts in as many as twenty countries and more than 100 years of experience in electric utility operations in the United States. The embassy worked with company executives to find ways to express how that experience was relevant to the UAE. In one particularly creative example, it worked in tandem with its sister embassy in Rabat to arrange a call from a senior official in Morocco—where CMS had been operating a highly successful power plant—to his counterpart in Abu Dhabi to offer firsthand testimony of CMS Energy's performance.

CMS Energy negotiators identified the strong points of the CMS proposal for the embassy, which worked them into the message. The message highlighted the proposal's technical and financial strengths, without denigrating the competition. It underscored other CMS strengths, including technology transfer, job creation, training and environmental protection, health and safety factors.

On the policy side, the embassy wanted to give the Emirates a reputation to live up to. American officials, the embassy said, should applaud the UAE's transparent bidding process, which would set an example for other countries in the region and ensure strong international interest in future privatizations in the Emirates. Last, the message touched on the importance of strengthening commercial and trade ties between the United States and the UAE to diversify the strategic relationship between the two—which until then had concentrated heavily on the defense sector and military-to-military contacts.

Tactical responses

Once developed, the strategy and the message had to be adapted to events and unforeseen circumstances that arose as the bidding process worked its way to a conclusion. The embassy provided CMS with timely and useful intelligence that helped the company respond to efforts by its foreign competitors.

Early in the bidding process, for instance, after the eight companies survived the prequalification process, the embassy learned that one of those eight—a British developer—had organized a privatization conference in the UAE. That conference would draw in all of the leading host-country decision makers. The embassy also learned that all of the speakers from outside the UAE would be British, and that the structure of the agenda seemed aimed at discrediting the experience of American companies in privatization.

The embassy quickly ensured attendence by its own representation at the conference and made arrangements for a senior official from CMS to be accorded a speaking role. Shortly after that, it arranged for Commerce Secretary Daley to visit the UAE on a swing through the region, to mitigate any potential damage from the conference.

Later, after the number of bidders had been narrowed down to three, the European consortium submitted a nonconforming bid in violation of the published rules. Some in CMS wanted to cry foul, and in the loudest voice. The embassy's advice was to stick with the original plan, congratulate the UAE authorities on the transparency and orderliness of the bidding process so far and emphasize the importance of keeping the process above reproach. CMS accepted the embassy's advice. That delicate touch in the end helped neutralize any standing that the nonconforming bid might have had and enabled CMS to preserve its good relationship with the authorities in UAE.

The embassy also helped CMS navigate the U.S. government's own complex advocacy rules. As mentioned, ADWEA had short-listed CMS and the French/Belgian consortium as the clear frontrunners in the bidding process. At the same time, another American firm received a different letter that permitted it to remain on the sidelines, even if it wasn't involved directly in negotiations with ADWEA.

Recognizing that the competition in reality had been narrowed to two, the embassy sought permission from the second American company to drop its earlier request for advocacy and give the embassy the ability to support CMS Energy exclusively. When the second company declined, the embassy and other U.S. government officials were left with having to advocate "generically" for American companies, rather than for CMS Energy as the clear front-runner—a potentially confusing message to host-country decision makers. The embassy took the initiative to work with the Advocacy Center and the legal offices at the Commerce and State Departments to refine its message so that it conformed fully to the advocacy guidelines yet clearly conveyed that the United States understood the bid dynamics.

Success

On September 30, 1998 Adwea announced that CMS Energy had been awarded the Al Taweelah A2 project. This news, Ambassador Litt commented, represented "a great success for post and for U.S. government advocacy efforts." CMS Energy's chief executive officer not only wrote to thank the ambassador and the other U.S. government officials involved but also made certain that its congressional representatives and the leadership of the relevant appropriations committees were aware of the role that the embassy had played.

The group that lost the contest to CMS, a French consortium led by Total and Tractebel, issued a stunning public statement acknowledging that the bidding process was fair and transparent. Total-Tractebel subsequently won the contract for the companion Al Taweelah A1 project.

CMS Energy has expanded its presence in the UAE and continues to operate the Al Taweelah A2 and another facility. Those investments have performed exceedingly well. The CMS presence in Abu Dhabi created and continues to sustain jobs in the United States. Returns on the CMS investment will flow back into the U.S. economy for decades to come. CMS Energy officials say Ambassador Litt's description of his embassy's work as a success is far too modest. They call the Al Taweelah advocacy effort one of the most well-conceived and well-executed examples of the advocacy process in practice, a model for future efforts by embassies worldwide.

AES in Bangladesh

CMS was a traditional utility that after deregulation looked abroad for new sources of growth. AES by contrast was an international company from its founding as Applied Energy Systems in 1981. By the late 1990s, when the events described below took place, the company had more than fifteen years' experience in the developing world, where more than half its revenues are generated.

Even so, AES was edgy about Asia. "We showed incredible discipline before the Asian financial crisis," said Ken Woodcock, senior vice president of AES. "Our Singapore office looked at all these deals" in south and southeast Asia "and said 'No, no, no, no, no.'" No deals with over-extended governments that might not be able to pay. No partnerships with leveraged real estate companies or quasi-governmental organizations run by somebody's cousin's brother-in-law. "Those deals we stayed out of ended badly."

But AES, which builds and operates energy systems around the world, wanted badly to be in the region. Just as the financial crisis that the AES Singapore office had foreseen swept across the region in mid-1997, the right opportunity showed up in Bangladesh. The World Bank Group and the Asian Development Bank had determined that power shortages cost Bangladesh at least one percentage point of economic growth per year, inhibiting development and impeding efforts to reduce the grinding poverty of much of the population. The World Bank and the ADB decided to address the problem by supporting construction of two greenfield thermal power-generation plants, a 360-megawatt plant at Haripur and a 450-megawatt plant at Meghnaghat. The plants would draw on the country's huge reserves of natural gas to produce electricity for industrial, agricultural and domestic use.

The projects would break new ground in Bangladesh by using private sector resources for the development of infrastructure—the contract winners would not just build but also operate and own the plants. Although the World Bank (through the International Finance Corporation, a Bank subsidiary that helps to finance and often takes equity in private-sector projects) and the ADB would support the financing, key to winning the contracts were three Bangladesh government entities: the Ministry of Industries that would lease the land, the Titas Gas Transmission and Distribution Company that would supply the gas and above all the Bangladesh Power Development Board (BPDB), the government-owned utility that would buy the power under a take-or-pay agreement.[1]

The government of Bangladesh faced some enormous challenges in sorting through the competition. The idea of privately owned power generation was entirely novel and not entirely trusted. Foreign ownership in particular aroused fear and suspicion. The scope and complexity of the projects, valued at $180 million (Haripur) and $300 million (Meghnaghat), were frankly intimidating to the bureaucracy, which was not much accustomed to deciding or even considering issues of such magnitude. Technical questions could take months to answer. Cautious civil servants sought frequent guidance from a political leadership that lacked technical expertise.

Briefing the embassy

AES turned early to the U.S. embassy in Dhaka for assistance and began what turned into a long and rewarding process of mutual education. Ambassador John Holzman met frequently with AES officials and conferred more often by telephone. "He challenged us on issues until he understood the problem," said Scott Kicker of AES, who did much of the negotiating for the company. "He stayed abreast of the situation, over many many months. When he was confident of the details, he would make our case to the government, and he passed the government's concerns to us." Ken Woodcock later commented that when AES corporate officers met with Holzman, they were astounded to discover that "he knew as much about our business as we did."

The principal competition facing AES in both projects was Marubeni Corporation, the Japanese industrial conglomerate. Marubeni could not match AES on price. AES was offering to sell power from the two plants to the BPDB at 2.7 cents and 3.2 cents per kilowatt hour respectively, prices well below those customarily charged in the region. But Marubeni had strong diplomatic backing from the government of Japan, which cited its foreign-aid program in support of the Marubeni bids. Japanese official development assistance to Bangladesh is so large, the government argued, that a Japanese company "deserves" to be awarded at least one of the energy projects.

The low AES price depended largely on efficiency in design and construction, which AES engineers believed would produce half again as much electricity per unit of fuel as any other gas-fired thermal plant in the country. AES was also willing to operate the plants at low margin. The government of Bangladesh, perhaps not quite believing in such aggressive pricing and unused to negotiating large infrastructure projects with private companies, appeared to worry that there was some catch in the proposal, some trick that, when exposed, would prove ruinous to whoever had approved the contract. Negotiations stalled.

Mobilizing resources

The situation called for a change of strategy. Holzman's growing understanding of the energy business led him to believe that if the decision makers in Bangladesh had the same base of knowledge that he had acquired, they would see the logic of the AES proposal in the same way that he did.

Over a period of several months, Holzman searched for ways to make the government of Bangladesh more knowledgeable about energy economics, regulation and the role of the private sector. With broad support in Washington, the embassy brought a variety of resources to bear: technical assistance supported by the Department of Energy and the U.S. Agency for International Development; extended visits to the United States for Bangladeshi mid-level officials under programs of the departments of State and Energy and the U.S. Information Agency, and high-level visits, including several by Energy Secretary Bill Richardson (who also came to Dhaka as U.S. ambassador to the

United Nations), culminating in a visit by President Bill Clinton in March 2000. Assistant Secretary of State for South Asian Affairs Karl F. (Rick) Inderfurth announced a new U.S.-Bangladesh Energy Partnership, led on the U.S. side by the Department of Energy, in 1999. A few months later, USAID and Energy folded the partnership into a new USAID program, the South Asia Regional Initiative for Energy and Development (SARI/Energy).

The U.S. efforts had a large and possibly decisive impact. "We can't wine and dine government officials the way our competitors can," said Scott Kicker. "But we can set up seminars and workshops on infrastructure development and energy pricing, we can set up exchange programs" to let Bangladeshi officials see for themselves how the challenges they face are handled in the United States, by the government and the private sector.

The negotiations that began in 1997 ended shortly after President Clinton's visit to Dhaka. AES won both contracts, with financing approved for Haripur in June 2000 and for Meghnaghat in April 2001. Meghnaghat began operations in October 2001, and Haripur in November 2002.

Weapons and defense

Building a strategy follows quite a different tack when defense equipment, especially major weapons systems, is at issue. Foreign policy considerations are very much out in the open. Major weapons sales require U.S. government approval, with several agencies and committees of Congress involved. The U.S. government wants to know to what uses any military equipment or technology it sells might be put, and whether any particular sale is likely to create dangerous regional imbalances.

From the buyer's point of view, the reliability of the United States as a supplier has to be taken into consideration. What is the risk to the buyer that shifts in the political environment will lead to changes in policy that might interrupt promised deliveries, scheduled training or the provision of spare parts? These political questions are part of the purchasing debate, as they should be.

Under these circumstances, commercial diplomacy and security policy overlap and become indistinguishable. Commercial diplomacy is put at the service of security as well as economic interests, and the embassy and Washington agencies must integrate business and political objectives seamlessly, so that they reinforce each other and multiply chances for success.

LOCKHEED MARTIN IN CHILE

The breakthrough sale of F-16 fighter jets to Chile in 2002 provides a case study. In 1977 the United States had effectively banned the sale of advanced weapons not just to Chile, then ruled by General Augusto Pinochet, but to all of Latin America. The Carter administration adopted the ban primarily to deny advanced arms to dictatorships and regimes with poor performance on human rights.

Twenty years later democratic governments were in place in nearly every Latin American country. President Pinochet had been forced from office in Chile in 1990. When Chile's democratic government decided it needed to modernize its air force, which then depended on aging F-5s, the United States under President Bill Clinton shifted ground. In August 1997, President Clinton announced that henceforth advanced arms sales to Latin America would be evaluated case by case. That decision opened the door for U.S. manufacturers to compete for Chile's business.

John O'Leary was deeply involved in this competition as the U.S. ambassador in Chile in 1998–2001. For him, the August 1997 policy shift made sense from every point of view. "The world, the Americas, Chile and the United States have changed dramatically over the last twenty-five years," he said. "The cold war is long gone. Summitry among thirty-four elected heads of state has succeeded general paternalism in setting the tone for hemispheric diplomacy. Democracy has returned to its historic home in Chile. And, in such a different political climate in the region, the United States, in military policy no less than in trade policy, now knows better than to define inter-American relations as 'one size fits all.'" O'Leary believed that "our success in the first application" of the new arms policy "depended, in substantial measure, on effective commercial diplomacy."

The embassy's efforts to promote U.S. aircraft for Chile's air force were initially complicated by the presence of two American companies in the field. Lockheed Martin was eager to find a new customer for the F-16, to keep its production line open. Boeing, whose stockholders had approved a merger with McDonnell Douglas only a month before Clinton announced the change in policy on Latin American arms sales, hoped to sell the McDonnell Douglas F/A-18. Both faced formidable competition from the French Mirage 2000 and the Swedish Gripen.

The embassy mounted a "buy American" campaign that did not discriminate between Boeing and Lockheed. Under O'Leary's predecessor, Gabriel Guerra-Mondragon, Deputy Chief of Mission Charles Shapiro (later ambassador to Venezuela) set up a system to ensure that information available to the embassy was shared equally and simultaneously with both companies. At the same time, Shapiro segregated inquiries from the companies, so that replies to queries from one company were handled in a private channel to which the other company had no access—a clever approach to the problem of the "assiduous firm" mentioned on page 14.

Building Chilean confidence in the United States required persistence and careful, high-level diplomacy. Defense Secretary William Cohen carried the U.S. message to Santiago in a visit to the Chilean capital in 1998. O'Leary writes that Cohen told the Chileans: "Whether and when Chile should modernize its air force to replace thirty-year-old fighter jets with new ones were decisions for Chileans to make for themselves. The United States took no position on either question. But, if and when Chile decided to buy new planes, we wanted to compete with France and Sweden to sell Chile planes made in the USA, planes that came with the promise of a thirty-year security relationship between the Chilean and the U.S. air forces."

At the same time, Cohen assured the Chileans that regardless of their decision, the United States would not waver in its support for Chilean democracy. His message, O'Leary says, was "we'll be with you" on the issues. "We wanted to persuade Chile that the aircraft buy is about more than aircraft—it's about a long-term strategic relationship" that neither France nor Sweden could offer. At the same time, O'Leary notes, the United States had to be extremely careful not to flaunt its power, which could provoke sufficiently broad public hostility to turn the government away from a U.S. supplier. Cohen aimed to persuade the Chileans that the United States would be a reliable supplier of U.S. weapons because the United States would be a reliable partner even if Chile bought elsewhere. The nuanced message was a welcome and probably necessary confidence-builder after twenty years of embargo.

Advocacy, while still necessary, became simpler after Boeing dropped out of the competition. The embassy and Lockheed Martin worked closely together, with the embassy handling the strategic and diplomatic aspects of the sale along the lines laid down by Secretary Cohen, while Lockheed Martin built the case for the F-16 as the best plane for the mission.

Despite the shift from embargo to case-by-case analysis, U.S. policy remained a constraint on sales. The United States, said President Clinton, will not introduce new and potentially destabilizing technology into the region. The F-16, it was agreed, was not new or potentially destabilizing technology. The Chilean air force, however, had some interest in equipping its new fighters with over-the-horizon missiles (called AMRAAM, for advanced medium-range air-to-air missiles) that could hit targets beyond the line of sight. No South American country publicly claimed possession of such weapons, and though it was widely believed in the intelligence community that Peru had AMRAAMs on MiG-19 aircraft it had acquired from Belarus, the United States did not want to be the first acknowledged supplier.

Neither the French nor the Swedes shared this self-imposed U.S. constraint. The Chilean press was filled with stories suggesting that the Chilean military considered AMRAAM an essential element in the aircraft decision. Under commercial pressure, the United States adjusted its policy. The United States, using a formula that it had earlier applied in Thailand, told Lockheed and the Chileans that the F-16s could be equipped to carry AMRAAM, though the United States would not supply the missiles unless and until another country in the region was definitively shown to have them.

It is possible that the press stories about the air force's insistence on AMRAAM were hyped, perhaps by French or Swedish vendors, or that the air force was confident that it could acquire the missiles in short order once Peru's true situation became more broadly known. In any event, the modified U.S. policy on AMRAAM bridged all the gaps. As O'Leary writes, "Chile could have bought either Mirage or Gripen aircraft from France or Sweden with such missiles or F-16s from the United States without them. Chile is not a bellicose country (it last went to war with another country in 1879). And its choice to take delivery of new aircraft, without delivery of such missiles but with a technical capacity to carry them should other countries introduce them elsewhere in the region, demonstrated a restraint that cannot have escaped the attention of its neighbors."

The change in American arms-export policy that made the Chilean sale possible was a bipartisan affair. The Clinton administration made the initial policy decision. The Bush administration confirmed it. Consultations with and formal notification to committees of Congress regarding the sale found strong support for the deal from conservative Senator Jesse Helms and liberal Senator Chris Dodd, both members of the Foreign Relations Committee.[2]

Chile's decision to buy American culminated a long period of diplomatic and political effort on both sides aimed at repairing a relationship deeply damaged by the tensions of the Pinochet era. Chile's decision had the support of both wings of the country's centrist coalition. The coalition's right conducted most of the negotiations during the presidency of Christian Democrat Eduardo Frei, and the coalition's left, in the person of Minister of Defense Michelle Bachelet, announced the decision in January 2002, during the presidency of Socialist Ricardo Lagos. It was, as O'Leary remarks, "an outcome that Salvador Allende and Richard Nixon would have found baffling, to say the least."

The outcome was entirely positive for both countries. For the United States, the ten aircraft sold will bring in about $600 million and help keep the F-16 in production (delivery begins in 2005). For Chile, as Secretary Cohen predicted, the deal has helped to lock in a vital strategic relationship, now bolstered by a free trade agreement signed in 2003. The partnership that the aircraft deal symbolizes and embodies should endure well beyond the thirty-year life of the aircraft.

Long-term planning

Building and then executing a strategy for a particular transaction can be immensely satisfying. The businessman and the diplomat both get to enjoy the moment when the deal closes and the fruit of so much labor is in hand.

Creating and conducting less focused strategies for the long term—what Secretary of State George Shultz called "gardening"—can be equally rewarding, even though the innovators and practitioners may not be around for the payoff.

SOUTHEAST ASIA IN GOOD TIMES AND BAD

Southeast Asia was and is fertile ground for commercial diplomacy with a long time horizon. Two-way trade between the United States and the ten countries in the Association of Southeast Asian Nations (ASEAN)[3] reached $120 billion in 2002, and U.S. direct investment entering the region in 2002 was valued at over $50 billion—compared to about $10 billion in direct investment flowing from the United States to China.

The United States as a matter of policy favors the development of strong regional institutions in southeast Asia. ASEAN, with common positions built on consensus, hopes to accomplish tasks that its members would have difficulty addressing on their own—adjustment to the stresses of globalization, development of balanced trade and economic relations with China and Japan, the peaceful negotiation of competing territorial claims in the South China Sea, and joint action against terrorism, drug trafficking, money laundering and other forms of transnational crime. As ASEAN develops, America's commercial presence in the region, as well as its military presence, helps to ensure that the nations of the region take U.S. views and interests into account.

This commercial presence did not arise spontaneously. American diplomats actively solicited its development, and American business leaders joined in. Paul Cleveland, ambassador to Malaysia in 1989–1992, played a key role.

As Cleveland tells the story, in late 1991, following a visit to Singapore by President George H.W. Bush, he and the U.S. ambassador to Singapore, former Indiana Governor Bob Orr, had a conversation about commercial promotion. The commercial programs in Kuala Lumpur and Singapore were strong: Cleveland's embassy in KL, and especially commercial counselor Paul Walters, had been instrumental in helping Motorola conclude its largest-yet single export sale.

But Cleveland and Orr were dissatisfied. America's biggest firms were coming, but others were missing an opportunity and jeopardizing their future. "Our view was that with globalization well underway, U.S. firms, particularly the large number of very substantial outfits below the threshold of the Fortune 500, needed to toughen themselves on southeast Asia's strong competition if they were to remain alive and well. Even at home in the United States, hard-nosed Asian competitors were increasingly taking business from our American companies." The embassies in southeast Asia, the ambassadors agreed, needed to "go home, tell American business about the challenge and opportunity, and bring them back out here to do business."

The idea that American ambassadors serving abroad should travel through the United States talking and listening to businessmen was—perhaps surprisingly—novel. Cleveland and Orr had no trouble securing support from their colleagues in the other ASEAN countries, or from the top of the Department of State.[4] But this was only agreement in principle, which means agreement without money. And as commercial and agricultural counselors sought to join in, along with representatives of the Departments of Commerce and State, the Export-Import Bank, the Overseas Private Investment Corporation, the Trade and Development Agency and other Washington agencies, the prospective cost began to look completely unmanageable.

But the private sector stepped in to rescue the government's idea. The U.S.-ASEAN Business Council, a Washington-based nonprofit whose members are private businesses interested in promoting trade and investments between the United States and ASEAN, offered to help out. After some hesitation—after all, this kind of public-private partnership had not been tried before—the ambassadors and the Department of State agreed.

Cleveland says "it turned out to be a great decision." United Airlines, Delta Airlines and Hyatt Hotels provided transport and lodging, and Council member companies set up speaking events for the ambassadors all over the country: Nike in Portland, United and McDonald's in Chicago, Delta and CNN in Atlanta, Fluor in Houston, the automakers in Detroit and a dinner that Chairman Hank Greenberg of American International Group (AIG) hosted with financial leaders in New York. There were press interviews and television appearances at every stop.

A United States Information Agency officer accompanied the ambassadors and sent press releases daily back to the embassies in the ASEAN capitals. Embassy press officers used the material with their contacts in the local media, to great effect. "We had thirty-seven stories—all positive—in the Malaysian press in just ten days' time," Cleveland recalls. "That was unprecedented."

The value of American investment in the region, and the value of American exports, rose dramatically in the years after the first trip. And the ASEAN Ambassadors Tour celebrated its tenth anniversary in June 2003, when American ambassadors and commercial counselors in Indonesia, Malaysia, Philippines, Singapore, Thailand and Vietnam visited San Diego, Los Angeles, Seattle, Detroit, New York and Washington, with support from the U.S.-ASEAN Business Council and member firms AIG, Boeing, Edison Mission Energy, Unocal, Qualcomm, United Airlines and Verizon.

The ambassadors' tour has certainly helped to strengthen commercial relations. Since the first tour in 1992, and despite the financial crisis the swept through the region in 1997–1999, U.S. exports to the region have nearly doubled, and at $42 billion in 2002 were roughly twice U.S. exports to China and three times those to Brazil. American direct investment flows have nearly tripled, from $17 billion in 1992 to $51 billion in 2001. And just as our commercial stake in ASEAN has grown, so has ASEAN's stake in American prosperity. The United States is ASEAN's number one overseas market, the destination of $78 billion in ASEAN exports in 2002.

The ASEAN ambassadors' tour was the first of its kind, but it is not unique. The Business Council for International Understanding, a New York-based private business association and a sponsor of this book, has hosted a series of similar tours by U.S. ambassadors in Middle Eastern countries (1994, 1997), Central Asia (1996) and the southern cone of

South America (1998, 2002). BCIU also brings ambassadors and other diplomats heading out to new posts into face-to-face contact with corporate leaders to share information and insights.

These visits receive nearly unanimous praise from the diplomats who travel and the businesses that receive them. The more that the worlds of business and diplomacy come together to understand each other's objectives, priorities, constraints and methods of operation, the more effective each can be in its own area of endeavor.

HARD TIMES: THAILAND AFTER THE CRASH

Commercial work is a lot more fun in good times than in bad. When developing countries were booming in the late 1980s and early 1990s, demand for U.S. goods and services increased every year, U.S. firms were eager to invest, and most countries were happy to receive their investment. This was the era of what the U.S. Department of Commerce called the "big emerging markets," the ten countries that Commerce Undersecretary Jeffrey Garten said "will change the face of global economics and politics."[5] The first ASEAN ambassadors' tour turned out to be a spin on a bandwagon, with eager participants jumping aboard at every stop.

The developing-country boom unraveled where it had begun, in southeast Asia. In July of 1997, Thailand's rising current-account deficit finally became too large to finance. Bangkok was forced to let the market, instead of the government, set the exchange rate for its currency. The Thai baht lost over half its value in a few weeks. Over the next eighteen months, the currency panic spread like an infectious disease, first to Indonesia, Malaysia, the Philippines and Korea, then to Russia and eastern and central Europe, and on to Turkey and Brazil. Exporters to these markets found that orders dried up. Lenders to these markets had to restructure their loans. Investors had their dollar-based balance sheets pounded down by new valuations. The suddenness of the changes was almost as dramatic as their extent.

Commercial diplomacy in Thailand over that period provides a case study in how to operate in good times and bad. Will Itoh took up his post as U.S. ambassador in Bangkok in early 1996 and stayed until 1999. He saw the boom, the bust and the beginning of the recovery, and led his embassy in aggressive commercial diplomacy throughout his tour of duty.

Boom

In 1996 the Thais firmly believed that the economic success of the previous two decades would continue, and even accelerate. The threat from Vietnam, which had directed resources and power to Thailand's military, receded when Vietnam withdrew from Cambodia and joined the Association of Southeast Asian Nations in 1995. Thailand celebrated the fiftieth anniversary of King Bhumipol's accession to the throne with plenty of pomp and circumstance. Queen Elizabeth and President Clinton made state visits.

American relations with Thailand began to turn more and more on economic issues, reflecting Thailand's growing economy and rising levels of U.S. business interest. Itoh had inherited a close working relationship between the embassy and the resident American business community, as represented by the American Chamber of Commerce (AmCham) in Thailand. That relationship was strengthened when the embassy accomplished two of the AmCham's long-standing goals, the conclusion of an agreement on civil aviation that expanded air service between the two countries, and signature—after fourteen years of negotiation—of a tax treaty that simplified tax planning and prevented double taxation of corporate income.

From his earliest meetings with the American business community, Itoh heard complaints about dealing with the Thai customs service. Itoh writes: "Duty schedules were often arbitrarily applied, and delays disadvantaged importers and customers alike. These practices effectively raised costs for Thai customers, some of whom were importing components or materials for value-added products to be eventually exported. In discussions with other ambassadors, the issue of customs reform was likewise a common theme among all those who represented Thailand's significant trading partners. Several ambassadors expressed the view that little could be done and reflected concerns that if they complained too loudly, reprisals could or would be taken against their national companies."

The United States, however, was able and willing to use some diplomatic leverage to come to grips with it. The U.S. embassy knew the Thai customs service well, through a technical assistance program that brought American customs officers to Thailand to help their counterparts introduce a computerized customs clearance process based on standardized tariff schedules. The embassy knew that there were many reform-minded individuals within the Thai service who found it difficult to take on an entrenched culture. The embassy resolved to use the U.S. position as a treaty ally of Thailand and, as Thailand's second-largest export market, to promote change in the Thai customs and to pursue other items on the bilateral economic and trade agenda.

Itoh sought support from embassies representing Thailand's leading trading partners for a broad-based coalition that would ratchet up the pressure on the Thais and reduce the chance that Thai Customs could harass products from firms of complaining countries. Sadly but typically, the European Union could not reach a common position. The French and the Dutch, however, joined in as national governments—though the Germans refused. The Koreans also came along.

When he called on the minister of finance and the director general of customs, Itoh was able to speak for the American business community, the United States and most of Thailand's major trading partners, whose ambassadors joined in. Hassling imports at the border, Itoh said, damaged Thailand's reputation as a safe and profitable destination for foreign investment and hurt Thai producers who depend on imported inputs. The arguments echoed the Thai reformers' and the collective approach with U.S. leadership helped tip the balance in their favor.

Bust

The World Bank called Thailand the world's fastest-growing economy in the 1985–94 decade. In the exuberance of the boom, the weak underpinnings of the financial system and the deterioration of Thailand's external accounts in 1996 and early 1997 went almost unnoticed. When in July 1997 the central bank canceled its promise to buy and sell baht at a fixed dollar price, foreigners and Thais were ill prepared for the shock. The baht plunged in value, and Thai companies with dollar-denominated debt saw their financial costs rise precipitously, to their dismay and ruin. Because much of the export sector depended on imported inputs, the gains from the devaluation were slow to be realized, while the losses came in a rush. The International Monetary Fund hurriedly put together a rescue package of $18 billion in new credits, but confidence was not so easily restored. The country slid into a deep recession.

The shock in Thailand quickly turned into an Asian financial crisis, as currencies in ASEAN partners Malaysia, Indonesia and the Philippines, and later Korea came under heavy pressure. American lenders and bondholders saw their assets dwindle, American exporters saw their markets dry up, American investors saw their balance sheets collapse. Commercial diplomacy became suddenly far more challenging but no less important.

Thai officials and Thailand's private sector developed deep suspicions of U.S. motives and intent. Malaysia's Prime Minister Mahathir publicly blamed "Jewish speculators." But the United States reached a judgment, which in hindsight proved correct, that the Thai government then in power was not capable of putting the country on a path to recovery. Despite heavy pressure, the United States refused to participate as a bilateral lender in an IMF bailout package in August 1997. The U.S. decision dealt U.S.-Thai relations a heavy blow.

The American business community and the embassy saw the need for a complete overhaul of their commercial diplomacy. The aggressive approach that used the leverage of the U.S. position as an investor and a market to promote policy reform would now be counterproductive. In a series of meetings, Ambassador Itoh and the board of governors of the AmCham undertook a thorough review of objectives, strategy and tactics. Itoh says the meetings were "marked by candor," which in diplospeak means they were unpleasant but ultimately rewarding.

The AmCham and the embassy decided that the first objective was to correct Thai perceptions of U.S. investors as quick-buck artists and the U.S. government as a fair-weather friend. That the embassy worked to improve Thai understanding of American business is not particularly remarkable—after all, that is part of the embassy's job. But the business community also worked to improve Thai understanding of American policy and the position of the American government. That was remarkable, and remarkably effective.

The embassy's approach to changing the image of U.S. business was creative and powerful. Trade missions, a common feature of export and investment promotion in 1996, had dried up entirely when the crisis took hold. Firms were unwilling to spend the money to come to Thailand when the prospects of business seemed so dim.[6] So the embassy, drawing on a trade-promotion technique Ambassador Itoh had seen work in Australia some years earlier, organized in-country trade missions. Full AmCham support helped recruit twenty companies to take part in the first in-country mission, which took executives of Bangkok-based U.S. firms on a three-day trip to the northern regions around Chiang Rai and Chiang Mai, with a day in Laos thrown in for good measure. Although the business participants found few new trade opportunities (though there were some surprises), Thai government officials were pleased, and the national media gave the trip coverage that Itoh says "helped convey the message that in a time of crisis Americans still valued the relationship and would do their best to help."

The first trip led to others. Itoh says: "Our successful Embassy-AmCham 'road shows' continued through the following year, when the new Chuan government was trying to convince outside investors that Thailand would soon make a comeback. Our schedule in 1998 included a one-day visit to the eastern seaboard, including an industrial estate that hosted several American firms, including recent arrivals Ford and General Motors. We also did a return trip to Chiang Rai and Chiang

Mai, this time with a larger contingent and an expanded program. Some forty-five participants signed up for a visit to the south, covering Surat Thani, Nakhon Si Thammarat, Songkhla and Hat Yai. Our final trip was over four days through northeastern Thailand, with stops in Khorat, Khon Kaen, Udorn, Nong Khai and finally across the Mekong River to Laos. Ambassador Wendy Chamberlin greeted us in Vientiane, noting that with twenty-five representatives of American companies, we were the largest American trade delegation to visit Laos in more than twenty-five years.... Three cabinet ministers participated in our last two trips. At a Government House reception, the prime minister mentioned our trip to the south, noting that no group of American businessmen had ever undertaken such a visit before. With the full support of the AmCham, we had successfully shown the flag to our mutual credit."

The business community reciprocated in dramatic fashion the embassy's efforts to restore its good reputation. At the end of 1997, when Thailand underwent a change of government, the embassy (with input from the AmCham) made the assessment that the new leadership had the experience, talent and popular support to reverse the economy's downward trajectory. Embassy reporting to Washington reflected that view, and AmCham companies in Bangkok began to sell a similar analysis to their home offices. Official visits from the United States picked up in number and level in the new year: in one five-day period in January 1998, the embassy welcomed Deputy Treasury Secretary Larry Summers, Secretary of Defense William Cohen and Senators John Kerry and William Roth.

But resentment of the U.S. failure to support Thailand with loans (as Mexico had been supported in December 1994) still rankled. The relationship needed a dramatic gesture to shift the context in which American actions would be viewed.

The American business community and the AmCham found a target of opportunity and hit it big. Former Secretary of State Henry Kissinger, in Phuket for a holiday, came to Bangkok in January at the urging of former Prime Minister Panyarachun Anand. Kissinger agreed to do a luncheon speech, but instead of a quiet boardroom affair, the AmCham organized a sit-down luncheon for 1,107 people in the ballroom of the splashy Hyatt Erawan Hotel. Kissinger's speech was just right for the occasion, reminding the Americans that Thailand stood with the United States in the days of the Vietnam War, and pledging to the Thais that America would stand by an old friend in difficult times. Kissinger joined Anand in launching "American Corporations for Thailand," to be funded by U.S. companies to support projects specifically designed to assist in the recovery from the Thai financial crisis.

From this beginning the visits escalated. Thailand's finance minister came to Washington and was invited into the oval office: Itoh says the picture of the meeting with President Clinton and Vice President Gore "was literally worth a thousand words" when it appeared in the Thai press. The prime minister followed the finance minister, and while the prime minister was in Washington President Clinton announced a $1.8 billion financial assistance package for an old friend and treaty ally. The package included funding for programs to strengthen U.S.-Thai military relations, extend the presence of the Peace Corps and provide scholarships for Thai students in the United States. But the bulk of the package served to strengthen American business prospects in Thailand, including $1 billion in Eximbank short-term trade finance, backing from OPIC (Overseas Private Investment Corporation) for two power plants and increased support for potential projects in Thailand from the Trade and Development Agency.

Commercial diplomacy in Thailand from 1996 through 1998 is a model of interaction and cooperation between the embassy and the business community. The benefits? A stronger American presence in Thailand and southeast Asia, deeper ties between the two countries, improved opportunities for U.S. trade and investment, and a more rapid return by Thailand to prosperity and growth.

Market access

No discussion of international trade and investment policy lasts for long before the appearance of the crowbar and the level playing field. The first represents the force and leverage needed to win concessions in negotiations.[1] The second is shorthand for a set of rules that is clear, public, stable and evenhandedly enforced. The two metaphors are easily mixed: it takes a strong crowbar to make sure the playing field is flat.

Trade policy is a constant topic of political debate in the United States, but the idea that trade policy follows a set of rules is not in question. Policy makers dealing with individual trade issues—for example, whether to raise tariffs on steel, or accept beef from Brazil, or give trade preferences to Central America, or lift quotas on textiles—operate within a domestic legal framework that provides due process for importers as well as exporters and builds on more than fifty years of international negotiations and international agreements.

The United States has been the prime mover in expanding the scope of international trade agreements. We have a great stake in ensuring that other signatories to these agreements share their obligations and are constrained by them in the same way we are, so that the rules that govern U.S. behavior in the international marketplace govern others as well.

American commercial diplomacy extends to promoting compliance with international rules as a matter of principle. When specific American commercial interests are at stake, this principle takes on urgency as well as importance.

Congress, which under the constitution has authority to regulate foreign commerce, has told the president that gaining equitable access to foreign markets is the most important trade policy task. The law is straightforward: "more open, equitable and reciprocal market access" is the first objective in any trade negotiation.[2]

To gain that objective at the policy level, U.S. negotiators have the leverage of the U.S. market itself. Protectionist or mercantilist nations pay a heavy price for maintaining their trade and investment barriers, if

U.S. negotiators make dismantling those barriers a firm condition for gaining access to the largest market in the world. That is why reciprocity—"I'll open my market if and when you open yours"—has been the core principle of U.S. trade policy since Franklin Roosevelt's first term.

Reciprocity implies fair play. Sharp practices must not deny to any party to a trade or investment agreement a real chance to make use of the opportunities that the agreement provides.

At the transaction level, commercial diplomacy can pry open markets with trade missions and trade fairs, export credits and credit guarantees, and other traditional tools of export promotion. But surprisingly often, the best crowbar that diplomacy has to move a deal to closure is simple high-level attention. Because the United States figures in such a large way in world affairs, relations with it are a matter of high priority to the political leadership of almost every country. When senior U.S. officials weigh in, good things often happen.

High-level attention

International trade rules, codified in the World Trade Organization, identify many types of protection. Nearly every country maintains long-standing trade barriers like tariffs that are bound at a maximum rate and may be reduced in global negotiations. Nearly every country has laws and regulations to impose standards of quality and safety on imports, as they do with respect to domestic production. WTO rules allow governments to impose special tariffs to offset unfair trade practices like dumping (selling goods abroad for less than they are sold at home, or for less than it costs to make them) and subsidization. The WTO also allows governments to impose temporary tariffs or quotas when a surge of imports injures a local industry.

All these forms of trade protection serve defined political, social and economic objectives, allowing countries, communities, industries and firms to cushion the worst shocks of adjustment to changing patterns of international competition. But legitimate trade measures can be abused to protect inefficient but politically important or politically connected enterprises.

GUARDIAN INDUSTRIES

Glass manufacturer Guardian Industries, a privately held, Michigan-based company with 19,000 employees and a presence in eighty international markets, knows its way around the world. The company is accustomed to trade conflict. The glass industry is highly concentrated and competitive. Guardian's advantages are strong management and advanced technology that produce a quality product at a low price.

When Guardian enters a new market, outmatched but entrenched local suppliers often turn to their governments for protection. According to Steve Farrar, a former foreign service officer who is Guardian's director for international business development, Guardian expects to confront protection and accepts it as part of the business—but the company counts on the U.S. government to make sure that the protectionist measures they face stay within the limits prescribed by international agreements. Farrar says the company's experience in southeast Asia provides some good examples.

Guardian moved into southeast Asia in the boom years. The company built a float-glass plant in Thailand, to take advantage of the reduced tariffs that the members of the ASEAN Free Trade Area (AFTA) are committed to provide to each other's products. The output of Guardian's Thailand factory easily met all the requirements as a product of Thailand, but the AFTA benefits were not so easy to realize.

Malaysia

In Malaysia, where Guardian had built a substantial market in the early 1990s, the local producer persuaded the government to impose a unique import duty structure on float glass—one based on shape. Rectangular float glass was hit with a duty of 65 sen per kilogram, about 50 percent of the value of more expensive glass or as much as the full value of cheaper glass. But float glass that was not rectangular was taxed at only 30 percent, with a preferential rate of 15 percent applied to imports from ASEAN countries.

Nearly all float glass that moves in world trade is rectangular and so faced the higher tariff. Of course, importers and exporters tried to beat the system. Glass was cut square (arguably, a square is not a rectangle), or notched at one corner, but Malaysian Customs soon ruled that these shapes were rectangular for duty purposes.

Under the AFTA, Malaysia's tariff on float glass from Thailand should have come down to a maximum of 30 percent by January 1, 1999, to 20 percent by January 1, 2000 and to 5 percent by January 1, 2003. But the "rectangular glass" provision kept the rate actually applied in the 50 to 100 percent range.

The Office of the U.S. Trade Representative included Malaysia's "rectangular glass" provision in its 1998 and 1999 lists of worldwide trade barriers, the National Trade Estimate report. The U.S. ambassador to Malaysia and the embassy's commercial officer pressed the government of Malaysia to kill the "rectangular glass" provision and meet its obligations. To signal the U.S. government's official interest, the embassy's commercial officer joined Guardian representatives in meetings with key Malaysian government officials. In the face of this pressure (and perhaps pressure from Thailand as well), the Malaysian government relented and brought the tariff rate into compliance with WTO and AFTA agreements.

Philippines

Local producers in the Philippines also tried to block Guardian's market access. Guardian began shipping float glass from its factory in Thailand to the Philippines in 1992. The Philippine manufacturer, Japanese-owned Asahi Glass, controlled 75 to 85 percent of the market and was well connected politically. Asahi Glass filed dumping charges in December 1993. The Philippine government opened an investigation and required importers to post a bond equal to 200 percent of the value of the glass, which could be forfeited if the government found later on that the glass had been dumped (that is, sold below normal value, defined in WTO agreements as the price the exporter charges in his home market or in other export markets, or the cost of production plus allowance for profit).

After three years of investigation, the government finally determined that no dumping had ever occurred—but failed to issue an order to end the bonding requirement, as WTO rules require. Embassy economic officers, who had monitored the case from the beginning, arranged a meeting between Guardian representatives and the Department of Finance. The clear signal of U.S. government interest helped to bring the Philippines around to lift the bonds and close the case.

A few months later—we are now in 1998—the local producer filed new dumping charges, threatening to start the whole process over again. The embassy made its interest known during the preliminary stages of the investigation, even attended several hearings. The Philippine Bureau of Import Services found insufficient evidence to pursue the case and never demanded the posting of bonds.

In April 2003, after glass from China had entered the Philippine market, Asahi Glass petitioned the government for temporary relief from imports of all float glass. The import surge, said the local producer, was causing serious injury. Guardian argued that its glass from Thailand should be exempt from any general protective measure, because shipments are small and relatively steady and do not contribute to any injury that may be found to exist. The embassy did not specifically endorse Guardian's position but did join Guardian representatives in meetings with Philippine government officials to urge that the investigation meet WTO standards.

The Philippine government imposed protective duties of about $50 per ton as a provisional measure in September 2003. Under WTO rules, measures of this type may be maintained provisionally for a time while the investigation proceeds; then a final decision must be taken. As the time expires, the embassy will be watching.

MOTOROLA

Of course companies are not always quick to ask for high-level intervention when they are trying to close a deal. A Motorola executive, for example, says that "seeking government assistance," especially from American embassies, "is not our default strategy."

Commercial diplomacy in the cellular telephone business is most often carried out at a highly technical level. Struggles to establish international standards are esoteric, long-term affairs conducted largely out of the public eye. Embassies, says Motorola, are rarely staffed with the expertise needed for engagement with these issues.

When competing for the business of private sector customers, Motorola likes to keep U.S. embassies and agencies informed but does not usually seek aggressive official support for its efforts. "We would rather work out our problems with customers cooperatively. It's difficult to use the U.S. government in problem-solving with a private buyer without appearing to apply pressure that can breed resentment later on."

But when a foreign government agency is the customer, bringing the U.S. government in seems far more appropriate. To analyze such cases, Motorola applies an informal checklist:
- Are Washington agencies supportive?
- Is the ambassador willing to engage on the issue?
- Is the commercial officer in country active and effective?
- Are there other sources of support we can draw on?

When PT Telkom, the government-controlled telephone company of Indonesia, changed the rules to prejudice a Motorola bid to supply a third-generation wireless telephone system, the company knew it needed a crowbar to level the playing field. The checklist checked out, and Motorola asked for help.

The PT Telkom tender had seemed straightforward. Motorola believed its bid was clearly superior to the competition, none of which was Indonesian. But as the date for awarding the contract approached, PT Telkom announced a change in the method by which bids would be evaluated. Motorola's bid, which was calibrated to the rules declared in the original tender, suddenly seemed at risk.

Motorola had no difficulty in establishing that Washington would support its bid. There were no other American contenders for the contract, and the United States was eager to promote commercial ties to the government of President Megawati Sukarnoputri. Ambassador Skip Boyce was ready to help, and Commercial Counselor Margaret Keshishian had good relations with decision makers at PT Telkom.

In the fall of 2002, as the date for a final decision drew near, Indonesian officials received a barrage of calls about the PT Telkom tender from Secretary of Commerce Don Evans, Deputy U.S. Trade Representative Jon Huntsman and other White House officials. Ambassador Boyce and his staff made clear to Indonesian officials up and down the decision chain that the U.S. government was aware of Motorola's bid and of the details of the late changes in the proposed method of evaluating the tenders. They also reiterated Washington's interest in the transparency of procurement as a matter of principle. And it is likely that President Megawati, still shaky in an office she had assumed barely a year earlier when the legislature forced her predecessor's resignation, had many reasons to care about American opinion.

PT Telkom awarded the $30 million contract to Motorola in early 2003. It would be wrong to say that commercial diplomacy produced the result: Motorola won the contract on the merits. But the vigorous U.S. diplomatic effort probably ensured that the merits prevailed. That would be a win not just for Motorola, and not just for PT Telkom and its customers, but for honest markets and fair dealing in southeast Asia.

Private sector action

Motorola's aversion to bringing the U.S. government into private sector negotiations is widely shared. American diplomats also shy away from intervening in private transactions, unless an international agreement is at issue or a vital national interest is at stake. But there are exceptions.

Soon after presenting his credentials in Santiago, Chile in 1989, Ambassador Tony Gillespie received a "cold call" from the chairman of a mid-sized technology firm in Georgia. Scientific Atlanta was a leader in antenna and ground station technology and, according to the chairman, was bidding on a contract to supply ground stations for the Chilean Telephone Company (Compania Telefonica de Chile—CTC). CTC had been privatized by the Pinochet government as part of Chile's economic transformation and was in the hands of an Australian investor. The government of Chile retained no interest in the company.

His caller told Gillespie that Scientific Atlanta had responded to an RFP and had reached a "short list" with NEC from Japan and Alcatel from France. The company had just been informed that its bid had failed on several points: it was to be eliminated from the competition. Scientific Atlanta told Gillespie they had never turned to the U.S. government before, but they questioned CTC's decision and the scoring of their bid as relayed to them. Something was wrong.

Gillespie was inclined to help, but this would be a fully private sector deal, with no government involvement on either side. After consulting his senior commercial officer, who provided background on both Scientific Atlanta and CTC, Gillespie contacted the American firm. In a lengthy conversation with a team in Atlanta clustered around a speakerphone, the company laid out the details of its bid and highlighted the points of contention.

With this information, and despite some reluctance on the part of his SCO to move into a private-to-private dispute, Gillespie decided go personally and directly to the top of CTC with a straight inquiry, realizing that he had little leverage other than that of his office. He called Mark Babidge, CTC's Australian CEO, who allowed that he had never talked to an American ambassador before, but who asked for details. Reading from his notes of the conversation with Scientific Atlanta, Gillespie laid out the company's concerns. Babidge promised to look into the matter and get back.

Gillespie was pleased to receive a call from the Australian a few days later. Babidge reported that there had indeed been "irregularities" in the bid scoring and that he had instructed his people to put Scientific Atlanta back into the competition. A few weeks later Gillespie received another call from Atlanta with word that Scientific Atlanta had won the bid and would be installing satellite antennas in remote Chilean locations for domestic phone service, with prospects for more business clearly ahead. Within minutes, Babidge called the ambassador with the same report and with thanks for having intervened.

SMALL AND BIG BUSINESS IN VIETNAM: ELLICOTT AND FORD

Ellicott

Small business can benefit from the high-level attention that large companies like Lockheed or Motorola, or large deals like the Baku-Tbilisi-Ceyhan pipeline, can easily attract. But small businesses sometimes feel they have no access to this source of support. How can a deal, or a company, worth just a few million dollars grab the attention of officials who have to worry about billions and trillions? One answer is that a modest transaction, if it involves a point of principle or has political significance, can take on the same policy importance as a billion-dollar transaction. Small businesses that find the principle at issue in their negotiations, and pursue it with energy and tenacity, can bring the government behind them.

Big companies may dominate U.S. merchandise trade, but as Jim Morrison, president of the Small Business Exporters Association, points out, 30 percent of U.S. exports are small-business exports. That is a hefty number. And Morrison says that small business is especially active in the most challenging and often neglected markets. For the United States, Canada and Mexico are the leading export destinations, but for small business exporters, they rank seventh and ninth, respectively. Helping small businesses secure export contracts strengthens America's employment base, reduces the current-account deficit and both broadens and deepens links between the United States and other countries. Small business deserves attention from America's commercial diplomats.

Small business doesn't need a big-budget operation. Peter Bowe, the president of a Baltimore company that manufactures dredges for clearing rivers and ports, explains how his firm has benefited from virtually cost-free U.S. government support. "We have four things going for us," he says. "We sell big-ticket items, generally to government-owned or government-controlled buyers, often in developing countries. And we have no U.S.-based competition in those markets."

Bowe's Ellicott Machine Corporation International has made sales around the world with U.S. government support. Very often, says Bowe, letters and visits from U.S. embassy officials and Commerce Department officers to foreign government officials responsible for purchasing decisions have a powerful impact. In a developing country, a U.S. government endorsement of a small exporter as a supplier "you should consider" can establish credibility. Ellicott, which has over a century of successful export experience, still benefits from that government endorsement, and lesser-known companies gain even more.

This kind of low-budget support helped Ellicott become the first U.S. supplier of capital equipment to post-war Vietnam. In 1994, soon after the United States lifted its trade embargo but well before the normalization of relations, Ellicott decided to compete for a sale to VINAWACO, the Vietnam Waterway Construction Corporation. The company was not entirely unknown in the market—Ellicott dredges sold to South Vietnam in the 1960s were still operating there thirty years later—but the labyrinthine communist bureaucracy was a mysterious and formidable obstacle. And financing was a problem. The U.S. Export-Import Bank was at that time barred by statute from doing business in Communist Vietnam.[3] Ellicott scrambled to assemble a creative but fairly expensive financing package for the $12 million deal, using an Australian bank that was one of the few Western banks then operating in Vietnam.

Some members of the Vietnamese leadership were eager to show that the country was open to U.S. suppliers, and the performance of Ellicott's dredges in the South had given the company a good reputation. But VINAWACO had little experience in international trade, and its officials were regulation-bound and cautious to a fault. Convincing them that buying from Ellicott would be a sound decision, politically and commercially as well as technically, was more than Ellicott, with fewer than 100 employees, could handle.

With the help of the U.S. Export Assistance Center (part of the U.S. Commercial Service) in Baltimore, Ellicott sought support from the U.S. government. The administration in Washington and the embassy in Hanoi wanted to show the Vietnamese, and the U.S. Congress and public, the advantages of moving rapidly toward normalization of relations. Ellicott's bid for help found an enthusiastic reception. Vietnamese officials began to hear from the U.S. Departments of Commerce, State and Transportation that Ellicott was a company "worthy of your most serious consideration" as a supplier to VINAWACO.

The decision to back Ellicott was no shot in the dark. The company was known in Washington. Ellicott had sold dredges to Mexico and Canada, and in 1994 Transportation Secretary Federico Peña visited Ellicott's plant near the Baltimore harbor to drum up support for the North American Free Trade Agreement (NAFTA), then before the Congress. Ellicott's employees included many members of the United Steelworkers union, and Peña lined up their endorsement. (Ellicott's USW local was one of the very few labor organizations to back the NAFTA accord.) Peña's visit was a success on both sides that helped to give the company and the government credibility with each other.

U.S. government support for Ellicott's bid in Vietnam included appeals at working and ministerial levels in multiple Vietnamese agencies. Then First Deputy Prime Minister (now Prime Minister) Phan Van Khai heard early and often from Secretary Peña, Commerce Secretary Ron Brown, Assistant Secretary of State Winston Lord and U.S. Ambassador in Hanoi Douglas "Pete" Peterson.

After nearly a year of effort, the contract cleared the hurdles in the Vietnamese Ministry of Transportation, which controlled VINAWACO. But without the ratification of a notary—an official of the Ministry of Justice with broad discretionary powers—final approval could not be secured. When the notary balked, Ambassador Peterson traveled from Hanoi to Haiphong to make a personal appeal. The contracts for the $12-million deal were finally signed in 1995, and the two dredges were delivered in 1996 and 1997.

Cabinet officers don't often get involved in $12-million deals. It's clear that the political significance of the opening to Vietnam gave this transaction attention and importance way beyond the norm. But as Peter Bowe explains, the principle of low-budget support to validate American exporters to government buyers in developing countries has broad application. Ellicott has benefited from such support to close deals in Venezuela, Ecuador, Mexico, Paraguay, Egypt, Indonesia, Yugoslavia, Jordan and elsewhere. The payback for the effort expended is hard to overstate. There are not many manufacturing jobs left in the heart of Baltimore, and here is a way the federal government can help to keep them, at the price of a few phone calls and letters.

Who could be against such a program? Some years ago a deputy secretary of commerce, who will be nameless here, turned down a request from Ellicott for a letter of support on a bid on a $25-million tender issued by a foreign government agency. "If we do it for you, we have to do it for everyone," Bowe was told, "and we're not set up for that." Why buy a postage stamp when you can pay unemployment compensation instead?

That cold reception may be part of a larger problem. The president of the Small Business Exporters Association, James Morrison, says that the members of his association lean heavily on commercial officers overseas—"a great resource"—but shy away from seeking contact with chiefs of mission or their deputies. "They're too exalted," Morrison says. Small business should junk that idea.

Export promotion isn't always cheap, but Peter Bowe finds that many of the government's more costly pro-export programs don't always serve small business well. Export credit, for example, has been a

48

long-standing problem. When official export-credit agencies in other countries offer soft, concessional loans to developing-country buyers, the U.S. Export-Import Bank has legal authority (which the administration for policy reasons may choose not to exercise) to draw on its "war chest" to match the competition. But that means a company like Ellicott often cannot put a good financing package together until its competitors have already acted, and then only if Ellicott is able to learn the details of the competing bids. For government agencies in developing countries, "how much down and how much a month" is often more important than the total price. Rules may need to change to make Exim more nimble; now, says Peter Bowe, by the time the bank reacts to the competition, the game may be over.

Ford

The same political motivations that engaged members of President Clinton's cabinet in selling marine dredges led U.S. government officials at all levels to urge U.S. companies to consider investing in Vietnam. But exporting and investing involve different degrees of commitment and risk.

For Peter Bowe and Ellicott Machine, Vietnam was a big deal and a good deal. They sold their product and they got paid. For some foreign investors, however, Vietnam has been a challenge. On paper the country is enormously attractive, with a young population of 80 million in an economy with one of the world's fastest growth rates. On the ground, however, investors find a bureaucracy unfamiliar with market economy norms or consultation with business. Investors must be nimble and patient, and U.S. government support must be persistent and patient with them.

American companies are aware of the risks in Vietnam, where the business environment in many respects compares unfavorably with some neighboring countries. Investments have been relatively few and relatively small. One of the largest U.S. investments is the Ford Motor Company assembly plant in Haidoung province, about 90 miles west of Hanoi.

Ford came to Vietnam in 1995 with strong encouragement, but no guarantees, from U.S. officials in Washington. As required by Vietnamese law, Ford formed a joint venture with a local partner, the Song Cong Diesel Company. The partners invested $102 million (three-quarters of which came from Ford) in a plant to assemble up to 15,000 Ford cars and trucks per year from kits imported from Asian sources.

Fifteen thousand vehicles is small change in the automotive industry. Ford produces nearly 7 million vehicles a year. But in Vietnam, where the market is about 40,000 vehicles a year, the Ford plant is a major factor.

Liam Benham of Ford Asia explains that for automakers seeking to sell in Vietnam, local assembly is essentially the only option. Vietnam is a closed market. The country is not yet a member of the World Trade Organization, and though it joined Asean in 1995, its participation in the Asean Free Trade Area remains quite limited. Vietnam does not yet give tariff preferences to cars and trucks made in other Asean countries.

Vietnam is legally free to be protectionist and uses tax and tariff policy to favor local auto production over imports. The country's "Automotive Industry Development Strategy" includes very high rates of duty on imported vehicles and relatively low rates of duty on component kits for local assembly. Beyond the tariff collected at the border, there is a Special Consumption Tax (SCT)—a domestically levied excise tax—set at 100 percent on imported cars and trucks but at only five percent on kits for assembly. The disparity between the 100-percent tax on finished vehicles and the 5-percent tax on kits led Ford and ten other companies, including market leader Toyota and number three producer Daewoo, to open assembly operations in joint ventures with Vietnamese companies.

By 2001 it was clear that Ford would have no quick payoff in Vietnam. Projections of rapid market growth to over 100,000 vehicles per year failed to materialize, partly because the country failed to build the roads, refineries, gas stations and other infrastructure needed to support a dynamic automotive industry. The eleven companies with auto manufacturing licenses could produce far more vehicles than the market could absorb. The Ford plant has never been run at better than 50 percent of capacity.

But the Vietnamese government seemed determined to make a bad situation worse. On December 4, 2002, Vice Prime Minister Nguyen Tan Dung, the country's top economic policy official, issued Decision 146, a decree that raised the tariff on imported kits from the range of 10 to 20 percent to 40 percent, effective January 1, 2003, with additional increases to follow. There had been no consultation with automakers or attempt to forewarn the industry that this blow was coming. With a single stroke, Decision 146 would destroy both Ford's cost structure and the demand for its product. It would add a 20 to 30 percent cost onto the price of a vehicle overnight.

Ford turned to the U.S. embassy and Ambassador Ray Burghardt for help. Burghardt was supportive and communicated quickly with the Vietnamese government, stating the obvious: abrupt policy changes undermine relationships with investors who have come into the country and frighten off those who might be thinking of investing in the future. Burghardt and his staff pressed the government to consult before acting, and on December 30 the decree was withdrawn.

But it was clear that this was not the end of the story. Two months later, in February 2003, the government issued "Decision X," a decree that focused on raising both the consumption tax and import tariff. For all automakers, Decision X was even worse than Decision 146.

In keeping with Ambassador Burghardt's strong advice to consult more, the government had issued Decision X in draft, with a final order supposedly to await consultation with the industry. But, says Benham, the industry's meetings with the government were monologues, not dialogues, and the government appeared determined to go ahead.

A chance encounter bought Ford some time. The Asia Society, a nonprofit U.S. educational foundation, was holding its annual corporate conference in Hanoi in March 2003, with the Ministry of Planning and Investment as the host. Deputy U.S. Trade Representative Jon Huntsman and Maria Cino, the director-general of the U.S. and Foreign Commercial Service, led the U.S. delegation. U.S. embassy and USTR officials arranged a meeting between Ford representatives and Huntsman and Cino, who immediately understood the magnitude of the issue and agreed to raise Ford's situation in their relevant bilateral meetings with Vietnamese officials. Soon after, it became clear that the government would not implement Decision X. The Huntsman/Cino interventions, along with continuing support from the U.S. Embassy, were believed to be key factors in persuading the government to think again.

Of course Huntsman and Cino went away as well, and by June 2003 the tax hike was back in yet another guise. Instead of an administratively decreed decision, the government—in this case the Ministry of Finance—this time sent a specific tax measure to the National Assembly for approval. The increase in the Special Consumption Tax on vehicles was duly passed by the assembly, buried deep in a long list of SCT amendments. The tax increase took effect on January 1, 2004, with predictable effect. Auto sales nationwide are down by 40 percent in the first quarter of 2004. Toyota has laid off one-fifth of its employees.

Is the story over? Not necessarily, not yet, though time is running out. Vietnam is planning for eventual trade liberalization, through both broader participation in the ASEAN Free-Trade Area and eventual accession to the World Trade Organization. Indeed the government justified its higher tariff on auto kits with a claim that narrowing the gap between the tariff on kits and the tariff on finished vehicles would ease the transition to AFTA and WTO. Ambassador Burghardt misses no chance to argue that tariffs and taxes should be harmonized down, not up.

Ford's story in Vietnam is inconclusive but instructive. It cautions U.S. officials not to oversell a risky business environment where a major U.S. investment may have a political payoff. It warns U.S. investors that their strategic planning has to account for tariff and tax walls that can go up as well as down. And it teaches that aggressive and well argued commercial diplomacy like Ambassador Burghardt's can buy valuable time to allow investors to adjust to changing situations and plan for the future.

Creating markets: USTDA

One U.S. government agency specializes in finding commercial solutions to problems of economic development—creating market access by creating markets. The U.S. Trade and Development Agency, with a budget of $50 million in FY 2004, is probably the smallest agency associated with either trade or development, but its work creates large opportunities for American exporters and investors.

USTDA is essentially a development agency, but its mission is to deliver development assistance through commercial avenues. It uses its own staff or U.S. contractors to bring private sector capital and expertise to bear on the classic problems of developing countries: infrastructure, governance and administration.

The agency works in emerging economies, broadly defined to include countries emerging from political crisis or natural disaster as well as from poverty. One part of the effort is identifying idle or underused assets that can be put to work—a harbor that needs a crane, an airport that needs a radar system, a power system that can be integrated across national borders. A second element is "trade capacity building," an ugly phrase that means strengthening the ability of countries to engage with the global economy and absorb what it has to offer. Technical assistance from USTDA and its contractors teaches governments how to make and improve the tools they need to function internationally: an open and transparent procurement system, a customs service, environmental regulation and enforcement, trade finance. According to agency director Thelma Askey, over 35 percent of the USTDA's projects result in U.S.

exports, and more than $35 of U.S. exports are associated with each dollar of USTDA project spending.

The agency is closely attuned to U.S. foreign policy priorities and often responds to appeals from American ambassadors and requests from other U.S. government agencies.

- After the signing of the Dayton Accords at the end of 1995 , the White House and the State Department asked USTDA to construct a plan for U.S. development assistance to the region. In Albania, for example, USTDA helped local authorities develop a s plan to invest in air traffic control equipment using revenue from overflight fees. The fees went into an escrow account dedicated to funding improvements to infrastructure—work that went largely to American contractors.

- In 2002, Washington agencies asked USTDA to identify ministries in Afghanistan that were most capable of working with the private sector. The agency and a U.S. contractor helped the telecommunications ministry create a system to design and request proposals, evaluate the bids and award contracts. The system does not favor U.S. firms, but U.S. bidders will find it familiar and easy to work with.

- In the newly independent country of Timor-Leste (East Timor), USTDA works closely with Ambassador Grover Rees to help the government build a profitable oil and gas industry. USTDA technical experts have been active in East Timor since 2002, working on development of a procurement process that is orderly, fair and transparent. The agency's work won praise from Prime Minister Mari Alkatiri, and the procurement process led to a successful bid by a consortium led by Conoco Phillips on a $1.2 billion liquefied natural gas project.

The agency opens markets for U.S. exports in another and fairly surprising way. The agency helps foreign governments prepare for trade negotiations with—the United States. There is nothing treasonable or even mildly sinister in the kind of technical assistance, which builds support for trade agreements in the private sectors of U.S. negotiating partners. For example, during talks on a U.S.-Central American free trade agreement (CAFTA), USTDA helped Central American and U.S. firms identify projects in the information-technology sector that would benefit from free trade. If and when the CAFTA enters into force, U.S. firms will be immediately ready to react to new procurement rules and opportunities.

Commercial aviation: Boeing

It's a common canard that the United States lavishes export-promotion effort and support on a very few large companies, while small businesses are left to fend for themselves. In fact the share of resources the U.S. Commercial Service of the Commerce Department devotes to small and medium-sized business and new-to-market firms is greater than those companies' share of U.S. exports.

The big company most often cited as the government's pet exporter is Boeing. And why not? The public interest served is strong. Aircraft design and manufacture is a strategic sector, and a global market is vital to commercial success. There are many reasons why commercial diplomacy attends so closely to the aircraft business. Here are just a few:

- U.S. exports of civilian aircraft, engines and parts totaled $53 billion in 2001, about 7.4 percent of all U.S. exports.[4]
- Boeing is America's largest exporter, with sales in 145 countries.[5]
- Boeing bought $23 billion in U.S. goods and services (2001).[6]
- Between 75 and 90 percent of the content of U.S. aircraft sold abroad is made in America.[7]
- The commercial aircraft industry employs 2 million Americans and accounts for 9 percent of U.S. gross domestic product.[8]

Export sales of U.S. aircraft have a great deal to do with America's prosperity. Put differently, the loss of U.S. aircraft exports means a decline in revenues to U.S. aircraft, aircraft engine and aircraft parts manufacturers. When corporate revenues fall, corporations cut costs, which means cuts in investment and payroll that radiate throughout the economy.

Boeing merged with McDonnell Douglas in 1997 to become the only U.S. manufacturer of heavy commercial aircraft. In the United States and around the world, Boeing (which is to say the U.S. commercial aircraft industry) competes against Airbus, which today is 80-percent owned by the European Aeronautic Defense and Space Company (EADS) and 20-percent by BAE Systems (the former British

Aerospace). EADS in turn is owned by a French state-owned company, a Spanish state-owned company, Germany's Daimler Chrysler and the public.

The Boeing-Airbus competition is a high-stakes game, but the United States doesn't always use its influence effectively. The heads of government of the European partners in Airbus are its aircraft's top salesmen. Laissez-faire is a French phrase but not a French attitude. The French president, like the German chancellor and the British prime minister, is quick to raise Airbus in conversations with counterparts from other countries. But perhaps because they believe that a company's offer should speak for itself, American presidents have generally been reluctant to get engaged. Raising commercial diplomacy to the White House level has historically been difficult and remains so today. Even at the cabinet level, U.S. aircraft exports in some cases have received less clear support than did Peter Bowe's dredges in Vietnam. The costs of this reticence can be high.

CANADA

When Tom Niles came to Canada as ambassador in 1985, the Canadian commercial fleet was very nearly 100 percent Boeing or McDonnell Douglas. Today it is 85 percent Airbus. What happened?

Among other elements in this sorry tale, the Canadian government, then owner of both Air Canada and Canadair, a Montreal manufacturer of parts for commercial and military aircraft, decided it could favor Airbus over U.S. aircraft without affecting Canada's relationship with the United States. And it was right.

The first big Airbus sale to Canada came in 1986, to a small and financially troubled charter carrier called Wardair after its bush-pilot founder, Max Ward. Wardair had signed a letter of intent to purchase ten Boeing B-767s when the company abruptly changed course and announced its decision to buy ten A-310 Airbus instead. Shortly thereafter, and not coincidentally, Wardair was awarded a new and highly desirable Toronto-Paris route.

That was an inducement that Boeing could not match, and that Airbus should not have been able to offer. As parties to the 1979 international Agreement on Trade in Civil Aircraft, the United States, the European Community and its member states, and Canada, had all agreed that aircraft purchasing decision should be made "on a competitive price, quality and delivery basis" and had pledged "to avoid attaching any inducements of any kind." But the direct relationship between the award of the route and the Airbus buy was never proven.

Wardair's decision was not the end of the story. Despite the route award, the company went bankrupt soon after making the commitment to Airbus, and the government of Canada, which guaranteed payment for the aircraft, ended up with several A-310s it really didn't need. Airbus gave the government a fairly easy out. It was after bigger game, namely Air Canada.

And it succeeded. Early in 1988, Canadair—at that time government owned but now part of Bombardier—won a fairly large, multi-year contract with Airbus to supply components for the A-330/340 program. The handwriting was on the wall. In May 1988, then state-owned Air Canada bought thirty-four Airbus aircraft for a reported $1.8 billion. The deal touched off rumors of multimillion dollar kickbacks that led to a police investigation that ended inconclusively in April 2003.[9]

Throughout this period, Britain's Margaret Thatcher, France's François Mitterrand and Germany's Helmut Kohl interceded again and again with Canadian Prime Minister Brian Mulroney on behalf of Airbus. Mitterrand, like Jacques Chirac after him, was pleased to be identified as Airbus's top salesman (his brother was president of the Airbus consortium), and Thatcher and Kohl of course were no shrinking violets. But President Ronald Reagan did not speak up for Boeing or McDonnell Douglas. Mulroney called Reagan frequently, often weekly, to push Canada's position on acid rain, fisheries, softwood lumber, pork or any of the scores of issues that at any moment are active between the two countries. But despite Ambassador Niles's urgings, President Reagan never took the opportunity to raise Air Canada and Boeing/McDonnell Douglas with Mulroney. White House aides told Niles that aircraft sales were "not a presidential issue."

Treasury Secretary James Baker did make a last-minute appeal in April 1988, but it was a done deal by then. Immediately after the Air Canada buy, Canadian (Canada's other major carrier[10] and the unsuccessful competitor against Wardair for the Toronto-Paris route in 1986) leased seventeen A-320s. And after the Wardair bankruptcy, Canadian received the coveted Toronto-Paris route.

PERSIAN GULF

A hands-off attitude was not a peculiarity of the Reagan administration. In 1991, after the Gulf War, Kuwait Airways rebuilt its fleet around the Airbus A-340.[11] President George H.W. Bush made no move to call the Emir to discuss aircraft or express support for Boeing or McDonnell Douglas. The Kuwait Airbus buy was a large contributing factor to the growth of Airbus in the Gulf, where it now dominates the inventory in most of the fleets.

The Clinton administration was more aggressive in using cabinet officers and the president himself to push big-ticket sales, at least in two highly publicized cases that involved intelligence information and intimations of bribery.

In 1995, President Clinton urged Saudi Arabia to choose U.S. civil aircraft. The Kingdom bought sixty-one Boeing and McDonnell Douglas planes, in what was then the largest aircraft purchase in the region's history. The French press at the time claimed that the award to Boeing and McDonnell Douglas came only after the U.S. government had acquired secret information about the Airbus bid, presumably through electronic eavesdropping. The "secret information" was widely believed to concern French efforts to bribe Saudi officials. An investigation by the European parliament—into the alleged spying, not the alleged bribery—was inconclusive.[12]

Investment access: pipeline consortium

Most of southeast Asia has eagerly recruited foreign investment for many years. The inflow of capital, technology, managerial expertise and market relationships that comes with foreign investment made the region, along with Taiwan, South Korea and Hong Kong, the great economic development success story of the 1980s and an example for China and India in the 1990s and beyond.

But the southeast Asian model does not have universal attraction. In many countries, entrepreneurial groups eager for foreign investment must engage in constant political struggles with more traditional forces that see foreign investment as a threat to sovereignty, to national pride and perhaps to their own position in society. These economic nationalists resist with extra fervor when foreigners seek to buy or develop natural resources that belong uniquely to the country and the land. In some cases—natural gas in Bangladesh, for example—sources of potential wealth remain untapped for generations, because the capital and the markets that could release them are foreign.

Ecuador is a poor country in a poor continent. A long history of bad governance and corruption have bred cynicism and despair. Per capita income is around $1,200, about 3 percent of what it is in the United States, and 70 percent of the population is below the poverty line.

Ecuador has important reserves of oil, first discovered by Texaco in 1967, but limited pipeline capacity to bring the oil to market. Periodic waves of hyperinflation, the most recent at the end of the 1990s, have wiped out savings and left the country without the domestic financial resources to invest and build for the future.

Occidental Petroleum was part of a consortium of international oil companies that proposed in 1991 to finance, build and operate a pipeline that would more than double the country's oil-transport capacity.[13] The pipeline would require an investment of $2.5 billion, about $1.5 billion to build the pipeline and another billion to fill it. For Ecuador it was a rare and highly attractive opportunity, but the size was almost overwhelming. Two and a half billion dollars was over 15 percent of Ecuador's gross domestic product. An investment of that size in the United States would be about $1.7 trillion. Pipeline backers estimated the project would provide 50,000 new jobs (employment for almost 14 percent of the labor force!) and revenue for the government of $2 million to $3 million per day.

Negotiations dragged on for years in an atmosphere of political turmoil. Governments changed rapidly, especially after 1996. President Abdala Bucaram fled the country to avoid impeachment. His successor, named by the Congress, served only sixteen months (he was later arrested for bribery). The next president, Jamal Mahuad, was elected and took office in August 1998 amid rapidly accelerating inflation and rising unemployment. Mahuad proposed sweeping reforms to privatize broad sectors of the economy, including partial privatization of the oil sector. In a dramatic move that some would call desperate, he asked the Congress to abolish Ecuador's currency and replace it with the U.S. dollar. But with the economy spiraling downward, a group of junior army officers organized a coup that forced him from office in January 2000. The coup leaders elevated Vice President Gustavo Noboa to the presidency, and Noboa's government completed the currency change within the month.

The Noboa government set a deadline for bids on the pipeline project. With the bids in and the deadline passed, the Ecuadoran army stepped in with a bid of its own, in conjunction with the Brazilian construction company Odebrecht. Occidental and the pipeline consortium cried foul. The American embassy complained in the strongest possible terms.

In challenging the commercial role of Ecuador's military the embassy was challenging a long tradition. Although foreign private capital—Texaco—built the country's original and only pipeline in 1972, a military government created the state-owned oil company now called Petroecuador, which took a 25-percent stake in the pipeline in

58

1974 and acquired full control when Texaco's lease expired in 1992. Oil and pipeline revenues directly or indirectly fund much of the army's budget, and many retired army officers find employment with Petroecuador.

The embassy drew on all its skills and powers and influence in its effort to cause the government to comply with its own rules. The economic and commercial counselors called on the ministers of finance and industry, and the political counselor worked the Congress. Ambassador Gwen Clare met one-on-one with the new president and talked extensively to the military establishment. The conversations were unusually blunt, and disagreements were brought out in the open.

Ambassador Clare believed then and now that despite the vehemence of the confrontation, the embassy was acting not only in the interests of U.S. commerce but in the interests of U.S.-Ecuador relations and of Ecuador itself. She hinged her argument on the controversial policy of dollarization, on which the government had embarked and from which it could not retreat.

Dollarization in theory would break inflation by linking growth in the money supply to growth in the country's net earnings of foreign exchange. In a similar way it would limit budget deficits: deficits could be no larger than the government's capacity to borrow dollars to finance them. But the same constraints that would kill inflation and balance the budget could stifle growth. Unless dollars flowed to Ecuador, the country's economy would stagnate or wither.

The embassy's line was clear and consistent: Ecuador's domestic savings are not adequate to supporting investment and growth. Without foreign investment, the embassy argued, Ecuador has no prospect of sustainable growth and, without transparency and a rule of law, no prospect of attracting and keeping foreign investment.

The embassy's arguments had intellectual force. They were grounded in sound economics and proven by example in many countries over many years. Backing up the intellectual argument was the economic strength of the United States, of which every Ecuadoran was aware. The currency conversion required at least a degree of U.S. support, especially in the International Monetary Fund and the other international financial institutions whose approval would be vital to the solvency of a dollarized Ecuador. A substantial portion of Ecuador's export earnings depended on trade preferences the United States could unilaterally withdraw, on Ecuadoran products like cut flowers and canned tuna and fruits and vegetables. When the embassy spoke, the government had reason to listen.

The embassy's determined and consistent efforts resonated with President Noboa, a civilian and in fact a market-oriented lawyer and academician. Perhaps more important, the argument seemed to impress the minister of defense and chairman of the joint chiefs of staff, both of whom, under the country's service-rotation system, happened at the time to be naval officers not associated with the army's late bid for the pipeline contract. The Noboa government signed the pipeline contract with the consortium in February 2001.

Complex barriers, patient persuasion

Motorola's sense that most embassies lack the expertise to handle highly technical issues is probably correct, but most is not all. The U.S. Mission to the European Union deals with a very large number and very wide variety of high-value trade and investment issues of great complexity, and it is staffed accordingly.

There is no lack of friction in U.S.-EU trade relations. Unresolved issues include EU refusal to import beef from cattle that have been treated with bovine growth hormone; EU restrictions on genetically modified organisms and foods containing them; U.S. tax breaks that allow reduced corporate income taxes on exports made through foreign sales corporations; a U.S. law that earmarks revenue from antidumping duties for the U.S. industry injured by the dumping; U.S. laws allowing persons claiming that their property in Cuba was expropriated by the Castro regime to bring suit in U.S. courts against foreign companies buying that property from third parties; and disputes over accounting rules, the association of geographic place names with certain foods and beverages, packaging and recycling regulations, customs and immigration measures against terrorism and on and on.

But the United States and the European Union are in fundamental agreement that freer flows of goods and services and capital will bring increased global prosperity. They agree that freer flows require transparent rules elaborated through negotiation and maintained by mutual interest. They work closely together, though not always in harmony. Their diplomats try to understand each other's position and political situation, so that each side can find the other's path of least resistance to a desired outcome. The relationship depends on the trust built up over decades of honest if contentious dealing.

In such circumstances applying political pressure to a market access dispute may only make matters worse. Chuck Ford, who as minister-counselor for commercial affairs ran commercial diplomacy at the U.S.

Mission to the European Union in Brussels from 1999 to 2003, points out that once political levels are involved, technocrats become entrenched, positions harden and the merits of the case may lose their relevance. Sometimes it's more effective to speak softly and carry no stick at all.

HARLEY-DAVIDSON IN THE EU

One such case involved a product with a tough-guy, big-stick image: Harley-Davidson motorcycles. In June 2000, the European Union's Commission, the EU's executive body, began drafting a regulation to keep young drivers off big bikes. The regulation would have made drivers' licenses invalid for those under twenty-four years old for motorcycles with engine displacement over 650 cubic centimeters.

Harley, of course, makes big bikes. The smallest engine on models exported to Europe was 883 cubic centimeters. Harley belonged to the Association of European Motorcycle Manufacturers, but the company was isolated in its opposition to the proposed regulation. Harley was not the only manufacturer potentially affected by the regulation—BMW and Honda both made bikes with big engines—but Harley was the only company producing only bikes with engines over 650 cc. So while BMW and Honda, which both had European factories, could still reach the eighteen- to twenty-four-year-old market with their smaller models, Harley-Davidson, which manufactured only in the United States, would have been frozen out completely.

Harley took its case to the Department of Commerce in Washington, which cranked up its formidable bureaucratic machinery: the International Trade Administration's Trade Compliance Center and Trade Development unit, the general counsel's office and the commercial service at the U.S. Mission to the European Union. The department wanted the mission to raise a formal complaint—in diplomatic terms, a written démarche—with EU authorities. But the mission had other ideas.

The draft regulation was still kicking around the working level at the commission. It was possible, after all, that the regulation's purpose was safety, not protectionism. If so, commission officials might be open to Harley's arguments and evidence that engine size is not a reliable proxy for performance factors like speed and torque, and that engine size and rider safety are not related.

Over the next few months, U.S. mission officers met repeatedly with commission technocrats in the transportation and foreign relations directorates, first of all to make the case that the regulation put Harley-

Davidson uniquely at risk. Commission officials agreed to meet with Harley representatives, who laid out their data.

The commission's real concern, it turned out, was not engine size but the ratio of power to weight. Even though Harley's bikes, and BMW's and Honda's, were within the power/weight limits the commission had in mind, commission officials believed that determined individuals could modify or downtune large engines to violate those limits and reduce rider safety.

But the U.S. mission's intervention had shifted the debate from engine size to power/weight ratios, and then to downtuning. What looked like a political issue had been rendered wholly technical. After discussions with the Association of European Motorcycle Manufacturers, the commission junked the engine-size provisions and instead levied a requirement on all producers to restrict downtuning. When the directive took effect, its impact on Harley-Davidson's sales was zero. The "on the merits" approach worked in this case because of factors that are not always present.

- First, Harley's performance. The company had good intelligence, acted promptly and backed up its claims with solid data. Harley learned early of the potential threat to its market access through its participation in the European trade association. It brought the problem to U.S. government's attention while the proposed rule was still under discussion at the working level, well before officials or interest groups developed personal or political stakes in the outcome. And Harley backed up its claims on safety with credible outside research.

- Second—and this is key—the proponents of the new regulation were in fact motivated by safety. Harley's sales were not their target. The fix was not in.[14]

- Third, the U.S. mission was experienced and well connected in the EU bureaucracy, with ready access in the directorates (departments) of transportation, trade and foreign affairs. The mission's officers, Americans and local nationals as well, had good relations with their counterparts. They were seen as problem solvers, not enforcers.

- Fourth, the U.S. mission's record of success gave it strength in Washington. When Harley-Davidson came to the Department of

Commerce, the first reaction was to overreact. The mission was able to write its own instructions because Washington recognized the mission's superior knowledge of the local scene and trusted its judgment.

PHARMACEUTICALS IN AUSTRIA

Market access for pharmaceuticals has an urgency that access for motorcycles does not. Depriving consumers of their Harleys may be foolish or misguided or protectionist, but it does them no obvious harm. Depriving consumers of medicine, however, may shorten lives or increase suffering.

Market access for innovative pharmaceuticals has been a long-standing problem in Austria, an outgrowth not of trade policy but of the health care system. The key obstacle is not certification or registration of a drug as safe and effective—a matter handled at the level of the European Union—but price.

In Austria's single-payer system, the cost of medicine is borne by a social security system, financed by premiums from compulsory insurance programs and by infusions from the treasury to cover deficits. An association of health insurance funds, the Hauptverband, sets prices and makes the decisions on reimbursements. Patients make a flat copayment of 4.35 euros (about $5.65), whether the cost of the prescription is 10 euros or ten times that.

A new pharmaceutical product that has passed its clinical trials and received EU registration has access to the market, but only hypothetically. As a practical matter there is no market in Austria for drugs not listed by the reimbursement agency. Negotiations over reimbursement may take months or even years. Meanwhile, patients have access to the product only if a chief insurance-fund physician grants a special authorization.

The reimbursement agency is an independent semigovernmental body. Although loosely subordinate to the Ministry of Women and Health, it is directed by a board that, following the Austrian system of "social partnership," includes representation from the Austrian chamber of commerce and the trade-union council. The social security system, which reimburses hospitals and physicians as well as pharmacies, has tended to focus its cost-control efforts on drugs, a politically soft target. That is why prices when established are typically 15 to 30 percent below the EU average. The disincentive to innovation is extremely strong.

Austria's research-based pharmaceutical industry has struggled with the issue for more than a decade. In 2002–2003, the industry association, the forum of research-based pharmaceutical companies (*Forum der forschenden pharmazeutischen Industrie*, or FOPI) did extensive qualitative and quantitative analysis, comparing drug prices and costs (such as margins for distributors and retailers) around the European Union. FOPI's analysis showed the extreme difficulty of introducing new medicines in Austria. Kristine Herzog of Eli Lilly's Austrian office, who was also FOPI's general secretary, called the study a solid foundation for a highly persuasive case for reform of pharmaceutical pricing and reimbursement.

But strong facts were not enough. The industry had great arguments, but it had no access. So weak was the industry's political position that even when a presumably pro-business conservative government took control in Vienna, industry representatives found themselves unable to get a hearing. "We tried for two years to see the head of the chamber of commerce and other key decision makers," said Herzog, "but we couldn't get in."

FOPI's leadership had passed from Wyeth and Merck to Lilly's managing director Alexander Mayr in September 2001. Mayr had excellent ties to the American Chamber of Commerce in Austria and to the U.S. embassy. He sought to use those links to build a communications strategy that could educate government officials and lead to a better environment for innovation over the long term.

The embassy was receptive. Lilly, Merck and others began to brief the ambassador (Kathryn Hall, later Lyons Brown, Jr.) on the Austrian health care system and the obstacles to innovative therapies. "We did not expect the embassy to handle the details of content," said Herzog, "but we did hope the ambassador could open some doors." JoeKaesshaeffer, the embassy's senior commercial officer, suggested that the pharmaceutical issue could be placed on the agenda of the bilateral "informal commercial exchange" (ICE) held annually between the U.S. commerce department and the Austrian ministry of economic affairs. "The ICE talks broke the ice for us," Herzog said. "It brought us high-level attention for the first time."

But the Ministry of Economic Affairs was a minor player in health care policy. Lilly and the rest of the industry needed a broader reach. With the Commerce Department and the embassy driving the process, the memorandum at the end of the ICE talks called for a follow-up meeting with a broader scope. "The ministries of economic affairs, finance and health, the reimbursement agency, and the Austrian chamber of commerce were all involved," said Herzog. "In the first year, 2001, it was not taken seriously, but in 2002 higher-level people became engaged. We had agreed minutes of the meeting and agreed 'next steps.' By the third year one or two key people from each organization were in attendance and we had real momentum."

The market access problem was not limited to U.S. companies, of course. But as often happens (for example, in the case of Occidental Petroleum in Ecuador, page 57), the United States took the lead because it has large interests and large influence and a pro-active diplomatic style. In Austria, at Kaesshaeffer's urging, the industry asked the American Chamber of Commerce in Austria to host a meeting with ambassadors from other countries with affected research-based pharmaceutical companies.[15] The United Kingdom, Germany, the Netherlands and Switzerland agreed to join the effort. "We are planning to have a multilateral roundtable with Austrian ministries in the first or second quarter of 2004," said Herzog. "We've come a long way in the past four years. Thanks to the embassy, we feel now that for the first time, we can talk to the key decision makers and our message has started to get through. Patients may soon have faster access to innovative medicines, and the industry may have fairer, EU-average prices."

Starting from scratch

The "level playing field" has become a cliché because it expresses a useful idea that has broad application. Broad, but not universal. In the post-communist world, where economies are shifting from organization by central planning to organization by market forces, trade and investment rules are only now emerging. These are societies with scant tradition of honest dealing between strangers, and not much sense of private property. Reciprocity of the usual kind is hard to envisage, much less achieve, when one side has trade and investment barriers based on rules and regulations that are public and that function, and the other side does not.

To follow the metaphor, until there are rules, there is no game and therefore no field to level. In this environment, American diplomats and businessmen alike have a responsibility to help build the playing field, not just to secure individual transactions, but to establish a basis for future growth and development in which all may share.

RUSSIA

Russia after the collapse of the Soviet Union was a crazy quilt of Soviet and post-Soviet laws and practices, torn by crime and violence, and prey to speculative fevers, hyperinflation and all manner of scams and sharp practices. Even so, many American businesses saw Russia as an opportunity, and the U.S. government, eager to place Russia firmly on a path of democratic, free-market development, wanted trade with it and investment in it to flourish.

Tom Pickering, who had already been ambassador to Nigeria, Israel, El Salvador and India, became ambassador to Russia less than two years after the end of the communist regime. The embassy had begun to build up a robust commercial section under his predecessor, former U.S. Trade Representative Robert Strauss, and Pickering reinforced the section by making sure that embassy officers in other sections paid attention and gave support to American business.

This was no lip-service effort. Despite the enormous range of issues confronting the embassy as the United States and Russia groped toward a new relationship in an almost unrecognizable geopolitical environment, Pickering spent roughly one-fourth of his time developing ideas and strategies for American business and cultivating business contacts.

Typical business problems in Russia, says Pickering, included finding ways to secure Russian government support and cooperation, stave off predatory tactics by Russians interested in taking over investments, assuring fair access to the market, dealing with often prohibitive and sometimes confiscatory taxes and tariffs, seeking consistency in changing regulations sometimes arbitrarily applied and simply finding a way to conduct business across eleven time zones and vast distances.

A few months before Pickering's arrival in Moscow, the United States had proposed to President Boris Yeltsin that a bilateral commission be developed under the chairmanship of the Russian prime minister and the American vice president to keep high-level attention on a wide range of issues where the two sides could cooperate to promote Russia's reform and development. The "Gore-Chernomyrdin Commission" inevitably became involved in commercial activities, including civilianizing Russia's defense industries, developing government-private partnerships for trade and investment, and addressing issues of market access.

Helping business take advantage of this forum became one of the embassy's goals. The embassy's commercial team recommended, and Ambassador Pickering enthusiastically agreed, to work on the leadership of an informal American business club to turn it into an American Chamber of Commerce. The business community responded, and the Moscow group soon became one of the fastest-growing and most effective AmChams in the world.

Russia was not a large trading partner, but it was a critical one. Washington lavished attention on the U.S.-Russian relationship, and the constant stream of visits by U.S. officials gave the AmCham and its members unique opportunities to be heard. The business community and the embassy both recognized that with close cooperation, they could become conduits for each other's thinking, in a position to enlist the highest levels of the U.S. government in commercial advocacy of the highest order.

The ambassador and the AmCham leadership thrashed out the most difficult issues at monthly breakfasts at the home of the commercial counselor. These roundtable sessions were a place to listen and learn and flag new and looming problems. For the business leaders, they were opportunities to hear the ambassador's views on the direction Russia was taking, not just on business issues but on democracy, security, foreign policy and the whole range of international and domestic affairs. For the ambassador, they were a chance to hear news and impressions from around Russia, from some of the most perceptive observers in the country. Out of these meetings emerged policy briefs and recommendations that were presented directly to the secretaries of state, commerce and treasury, senators and representatives, and on their frequent trips to Russia, to the vice president and president as well.

While the Moscow embassy worked with the business community to move its concerns to the top of the U.S.-Russia bilateral agenda, more traditional approaches to commercial diplomacy were not neglected. The embassy made frequent approaches to the new Russian leadership to raise both specific cases and general business problems. One area that demanded and received a great deal of attention was the rights of minority investors, who were frequently the dupes of crude but effective, and generally legal, asset-stripping schemes.

In one of these quasi-swindles, a foreign investor, looking for a local partner who could steer him through the minefield of Russia's half-formed capitalism, would link up with a one of the many "biznezmeni" who offered good connections and an understanding of how Russia works. The foreigner might acquire a substantial stake in a Russian company, but not a majority of the voting shares. The Russian partners would then use their control to transfer the valuable assets of the company to another company that they controlled entirely, leaving the foreign minority investor with a hollowed-out shell. The ability of the biznezmeni (often former communist apparatchiks) to arrange favorable interpretations of, or changes in, laws and regulations left many foreign investors with no recourse.

The embassy developed a program to frustrate these swindles. At the front end was active counseling to American investors, with simple guidelines: know your partner, know your local government and find effective ways to deal with the central government in Moscow. This word of warning was often enough to send a saving jolt of prudence through the mindset of investors who might have been too eager to enter a new market.

At the same time the embassy and the AmCham reached out to the Russians. The AmCham, which by the mid-1990s numbered more than 600 American companies, invited Russians to speak to its membership. That would be no big deal in most of the world, of course, but for many Russian business leaders and government officials, mixing with foreigners and taking questions were new experiences. It was through the Chamber that many of the new biznezmeni, who had been fond of comparing themselves to the Jim Fisks and Jay Goulds of America's robber-baron era, learned that their fast-and-loose practices would not be tolerated. It was not a lesson that went down well, or easily, but with time and persistence—two essentials of diplomacy—Russian understanding of the nexus between capitalism and law began to deepen.

Central Asia

The U.S. Embassy in Kazakhstan faced similar problems in a more primitive setting. Elizabeth Jones, ambassador in Almaty from 1995 to 1998, likes to talk about her generic and specific commercial diplomacy—helping establish the norms of commercial behavior, and protecting the interests of American companies.

Kazakhstan for many reasons wanted to establish its independence from Russia, not just in name but in practice. The regime adopted early accession to the World Trade Organization as a national goal, and much of U.S. generic commercial diplomacy was framed with WTO requirements in mind.[16] In addition to the usual embassy staff of economic, commercial and agricultural officers, Ambassador Jones could draw on technical support from the Treasury Department and, especially, the Agency for International Development (USAID). Nongovernmental organizations like Transparency International, the private, European-based coalition against corruption, were also extremely helpful.

The United States provided Kazakhstan with advice and assistance on construction of the legal system, including seminars by jurists on judicial, legislative and executive-branch ethics and instruction on the role of precedent in Western law. (The Soviet Union relied less on precedent than on "telephone justice"—a phone call to the judge from a Party official). Kazakhstan needed help in developing accountancy (not the fine points but the basic concepts), tax codes, a monetary system and a central bank, budget systems, banking regulations, corporate law, a stock exchange, contract law, public tendering, a customs service—the list seemed endless. Directly and indirectly, the embassy supported training for officials and private entrepreneurs. One major program aimed at helping small businesses start up and take root across the country.

Western countries shared these interests, and Western embassies worked cooperatively on issues like taxation, insurance, customs regulations and the like. This cooperation was especially strong in the energy area. The opportunity to develop Kazakhstan's vast oil and gas reserves, some of the world's largest, attracted virtually every major player in the international energy and pipeline sector. Western bidders on major projects like development of the Kashagan oilfield, with reserves greater than those of the United States, formed consortia in which United States, European and often Asian and Middle Eastern firms were allied.

Behind all this activity is the belief that implanting Western ways of doing business will bring Kazakhstan into the global economy, raising the country's stake in maintaining a stable, peaceful and open society that can attract foreign investment and increase its prosperity. That in turn will promote geopolitical stability in a part of the world where levels of political uncertainty are extremely high.

Rules

The basic rules of international trade were written not so long ago. Twenty-three countries negotiated and signed the General Agreement on Tariffs and Trade (GATT) at conferences in Havana and Geneva in 1947. The authors of the GATT intended the document as a kind of charter for an International Trade Organization that would take its place beside the International Monetary Fund and the International Bank for Reconstruction and Development (World Bank) as pillars of a new postwar international economic order.

Things did not work out that way. Opposition in the U.S. Congress persuaded the Truman administration to defer indefinitely the submission of the GATT to the Senate for ratification. The United States signed the GATT in 1947, but in the United States the document never had treaty status or the force of law. Without U.S. participation, an International Trade Organization would have no point, and other countries did not pursue it. Diplomats improvised a GATT secretariat and elected a director general to keep the agreement alive and make it function.

The International Trade Organization conceived in 1947 was finally born as the World Trade Organization in 1994. Over the forty-seven years of gestation, international trade rules grew from the thirty-four articles and fifty-two pages of the original GATT to the forty-six agreements, understandings and decisions, in 739 pages, of the Final Act of April 15, 1994. And the number of signatories grew from the founding twenty-three to 146.

U.S. trade law has grown even more rapidly. The original antidumping act, for example, was two pages of text. Now antidumping laws take up well over 100 pages in the statute books.[1] The North American Free Trade Agreement is five fat volumes of text and tables, much of it devoted to rules for determining the country of origin of different kinds of products.

As rich as trade law is, it is only part of the body of international law affecting commercial relationships. Commercial diplomacy must concern itself with the rules of the World Trade Organization, the World Intellectual Property Organization, the International Maritime

Organization, the International Telecommunication Union, the World Customs Organization, the Berne and Lisbon conventions, the International Center for the Settlement of Investment Disputes, the Universal Commercial Code and a score of other organizations, treaties, conventions and agreements. And commercial diplomacy gets into local law and administration as well. Are local regulations skewed to favor certain commercial results? Do local authorities treat all companies equally? Do local authorities solicit bribes, or take them when offered?

Good rules make international economic relationships far more stable and predictable. They reduce costs by lowering risk. Investors need predictability. When rules are skirted or ignored, risks and costs go up and welfare suffers. The negotiation, interpretation, application and enforcement of international rules is a growing part of commercial diplomacy.

Property

The notion of property underlies all of the rules that govern trade and investment. Without property and ownership, there is no market in which to trade and no purpose or incentive to investment.

Physical property and property rights have been well understood since capitalism replaced feudalism as the organizing principle of Western societies. U.S. diplomats have worked to protect American property abroad from the earliest days of the republic.

In recent years, information and the product of the mind have become sources of wealth at least equal to the output of farm or factory. Intellectual property is as important economically as physical property. Lester Thurow writes: "Knowledge does not come free. Investments have to be made to extract it. Just as gold miners do not mine gold unless they will be allowed to keep the gold they extract, so intellectual miners do not mine knowledge unless they are allowed to keep the knowledge they extract." And in a globalized world, where capital, raw materials and (increasingly) labor are available to all competitors at the same price, "the only remaining sources of true competitive advantage are technologies that others do not have, copyrights they cannot infringe or brand names that set one apart. None of these is possible without systems for protecting patents, copyrights and trademarks."[2]

The American stake in intellectual property rights has grown enormously over the past quarter century. Copyright industries alone have increased their contribution to American GDP from $43 billion or 2.2 percent in 1977, to $535 billion or 5.2 percent in 2001.[3] Export revenues earned by the recording, motion picture, software and print industries reached about $90 billion in 2001.[4] The U.S. Customs Service estimates that counterfeiting activity costs the U.S. more than $200 billion annually and has resulted in the loss of 750,000 American jobs.[5] The value of U.S.-owned trademarks like Budweiser™, Ford™, Windows™ or Coke™ has not been calculated and may not be calculable, but it is surely in hundreds of billions of dollars.

These properties are easy targets. A dark soft drink in a bottle with a bright red label and a white-letter script coasts on the brand image that the Coca-Cola Company has spent decades and hundreds of millions of dollars to build. Films, tapes and recordings are easily copied without authorization and without much loss of quality. Consumers may not know the difference between what they buy and the real thing, or they may know and not care.

Fifty years ago, the various international conventions and agreements that provided mutual recognition and protection of patents, copyrights and trademarks often lacked broadly accepted standards and were difficult to enforce. U.S. policymakers and owners of intellectual property noted the contrast with the General Agreement on Tariffs and Trade, dealing with trade in goods, which had a common set of rules and agreed mechanisms for settling disputes and rebalancing concessions. Beginning in the 1970s, the United States began to raise protection of intellectual property as an issue in trade negotiations. With U.S. leadership, in 1994 an agreement on intellectual property[6] became part of the system of the World Trade Organization, and American embassies had a strong body of international law to work with.

But protection of intellectual property isn't just legal maneuver. Violations seem especially common in developing countries where legal protections are spotty. Finding the diplomatic path that will secure a host government's cooperation is a tricky business. A soft request will rarely suffice: for political leaders in the developing world, not to mention for their bureaucracies, defending Mickey Mouse or Microsoft is not exactly a priority. The big stick poses other problems: Resort to the pressures of trade sanctions may bring short-term successes but can leave a residue of ill-will that imposes costs in other areas. Embassies out to secure intellectual property rights need good judgment, local knowledge, energy and imagination.

PLANNING AND PERSUASION: PROCTER & GAMBLE IN CHINA

Procter & Gamble was one of the first American consumer-products firms to enter China after the normalization of diplomatic relations in 1978. P&G has seen China's economy change from rigid central planning marked by grinding poverty and frequent famines to rapid, turbulent and often chaotic growth that has no match or model in world history. China's transformation has brought with it political and social strains that the regime has tried as much to suppress as to accommodate. And in the gaps between the exhausted norms of the autarkic communist past, and the untried laws and regulations of the market-based, international future, there is plenty of room for reckless behavior.

Procter & Gamble, like many other Western companies in China, faces challenges generated by its own success. Among the most serious and debilitating is counterfeiting, the unauthorized use of P&G trademarks, labels, brand names and the like to disguise imitation products as the real thing. Counterfeit goods, often so shoddy as to be worthless or even harmful to the consumer, steal market share and undercut margins. Much more dangerous, they drain legitimate brands of value built up over many years. Procter & Gamble estimates that in the year 2000, its losses due to counterfeiting in China amounted to $150 million.

Procter & Gamble's fight against counterfeiting in China began at the top, in the chairman's office. John Pepper, P&G's CEO from 1995 to 1999 and chairman until 2002, believed (and believes) that a strong presence in China's burgeoning market is essential to the continued strength of Procter & Gamble in the 21st century. He believed (and believes) as well that the rules that have allowed global trade to expand at twice the rate of global output over the past fifty years will prove to be as important to China's welfare as they have been to America's, or Europe's or Japan's.

With leadership from the chairman, Procter & Gamble sought out other companies that faced similar problems in China. P&G's intent was to build a broad business coalition that would approach the Chinese government in a cooperative spirit to seek support for a crackdown on counterfeiters. The Quality Brand Protection Committee (QBPC) came together in 1999 and grew in fairly short order to more than eighty member companies. The breadth of the QBPC was notable in the range of industries represented and in the nationalities of the parent members: firms from the United States, Europe, Japan, Hong Kong and elsewhere in consumer products, pharmaceuticals, electronics, auto parts, medical supplies—wherever branding establishes quality and creates equity value.

Procter & Gamble and the QBPC sought support and counsel from the U.S. embassy. The embassy, of course, was deeply engaged with the Chinese government on the issue of China's accession to the World

Trade Organization, and intellectual property issues were a critical element in those negotiations. John Pepper met with Ambassador Joseph Prueher in 2000 and with Ambassador Clark Randt beginning in 2001. The embassy formed an intellectual property rights working group, which included the senior economic, commercial and trade policy officers. This "IPR Committee" took on counterfeiting and began to meet regularly with key companies and with the QBPC.

From the beginning of their discussions, the QBPC and the embassy had no disagreement over tactics. The businessmen and the diplomats, all experienced in China, knew that heavyhanded tactics would not work. Confrontation would only promote Chinese resistance, and without active engagement of the Chinese government, nothing could be accomplished.

The embassy and the QBPC resolved to keep the issue international and, to the extent possible, apolitical. They agreed to deal with the Chinese government in a coordinated but separate way, so as not to confound business interests with geopolitical tensions or other areas of diplomatic stress.

The QBPC stayed within the communication channels that China's Ministry of Foreign Trade and Economic Development (MOFTEC) had established for foreign companies to contain and routinize foreign business pressure on the creaky and erratic regulatory system. The QBPC set itself up as a subcommittee of the China Association of Enterprises with Foreign Investment (CAEFI), an officially recognized go-between for foreign investors facing difficulties or needing help with the Chinese government. Its official status gave Chinese bureaucrats the confidence to deal with the QBPC in a more open and open-minded way.

The embassy and its IPR committee brought in counterparts from other embassies, which also had been approached by the QBPC and its member firms. The Japanese embassy was especially active. This careful diplomacy by the companies and the embassies allowed the anticounterfeiting coalition to retain access to Chinese officials even when incidents like the bombing of the Chinese embassy in Belgrade or the deadly skirmish between a U.S. surveillance aircraft and a Chinese fighter chilled official relations for a time.

The embassy and the business community maintained close coordination while avoiding joint forays into the Chinese government. Embassy personnel attended QBPC meetings and QBPC members helped train junior officers. Position papers were exchanged. Advice from the business community helped the embassy to organize seminars and direct visitor grants to educate Chinese officials about the issue.

But all this subtle strategy might have accomplished little or nothing if China's leadership had not been intent on joining the World Trade Organization. Beijing's determination created the leverage the United States and other countries could use to influence Chinese policy. It created as well the top-down pressure that caused Chinese bureaucrats to respond to instruction—which is not always the case. And the success of a few Chinese firms in building brand equity of their own created a small, but powerful and growing, domestic interest in tougher and more effective anticounterfeiting programs.

In 1999 P&G's top man in China, John Yam, could scarcely get a hearing with government officials on counterfeiting. In August 2003, he and some of his QBPC colleagues spent two and half hours with Vice Premier Wu Yi, the top Chinese government leader in charge of anticounterfeiting. The vice premier, who led an interministerial anticounterfeiting task force, asked the Ministry of Commerce to set up regular meetings with QBPC to deal with the counterfeit problem.

Diplomatic and business efforts shook China's attitude toward counterfeiting. What once was a problem that could be ignored has become a problem that must be addressed. For Procter & Gamble , and no doubt for other firms as well, the gains have been dramatic. Procter & Gamble estimates its losses due to counterfeiting have fallen from around $150 million in 2000 to $100 million in 2003 and continue to decline. The investment of effort by P&G and the American government is paying a handsome return.

Showmanship: Mars and Estée Lauder

Mars Incorporated launched its famous M&Ms chocolate candies in China in 1990, in connection with the Asian Games. Within months, the famous M&M trademark came under assault by a Chinese company that was turning out candies called "W&W," in packaging identical to M&Ms. Adding injury to insult, the Chinese candy was close to inedible. W&W not only stole the M&M mark, it was devaluing the brand with each appalling bag.

Estée Lauder had a slightly different problem in Indonesia. The company counts on the power of its famous name and trademark to attract customers in new markets, where the mark is known even before the product reaches the shelves. But in Indonesia in the boom years of the early 1990s, local entrepreneurs, eager to identify their products with anything Western, took famous marks and slapped them randomly on all sorts of stuff. In Jakarta you could get your jitney rolling on Estée Lauder tires; in Surabaya you could fight mosquitoes with Estée insecticide. The image that Estée Lauder wanted its name to bring to its customers' minds was very much at risk.

Mars had registered the M&M mark in China, but efforts to defend the mark in local courts, when successful were not enforced. In Indonesia, officials at the underfunded Directorate General for Intellectual Property claimed not to know of Estée Lauder. Both companies could have pushed the U.S. government to escalate the legal dispute, but they chose a different tack.

Mars put together a coffee-table book of all the company's famous marks—M&M™, Snickers™, Milky Way™, Uncle Ben's™, Whiskas™ and the rest—and together with Ambassador J. Stapleton Roy delivered the book to the director of China's patent and trademark office. The ambassador used the opportunity to make a full presentation on the importance of trademarks and their protection, for the benefit of the consumer as well as the trademark owner. The presentation dealt with broad issues at the level of principle, without reference to M&M or to U.S. trademarks. People in the room described it as educational, not aggressive. And the fact that the ambassador, who enjoyed great respect in China, engaged himself personally and devoted extended time to the issue made a deep impression on the Chinese officials. Mars noticed a sharp improvement in official Chinese support for enforcement of trademark rights following Ambassador Roy's presentation.

In Indonesia, Estée Lauder also put together a book of its marks and products and joined Ambassador Bob Barry in presenting it to Nico Kansil, director general of the intellectual property office.[7] The ambassador made a carefully prepared presentation that placed Estée Lauder's problem in the context of international trademark law, eliciting expressions of Indonesia's support for the general principles of mutual recognition and protection of famous trademarks.

Not just Mars and Estée Lauder but all trademark holders benefited. The two cases showed what good diplomats know: governments respond better to an appeal based on a broadly accepted principle than to an argument based on the situation of a single firm. Once there is agreement on the principle, finding a solution becomes a practical or technical problem from which political tension has been largely drained.

SHAKING THINGS UP: PROPERTY RIGHTS IN PARAGUAY

The careful, coordinated approach is not a diplomatic template for all locales or seasons. Sometimes the situation calls for a much harder stance, with much more aggressive intervention. But the decision to get tough is rarely easy.

When an ambassador and an embassy look at the tactics to use in any given case, they must ask themselves, "How far can we go?" When does advocacy become so intense or so shrill that other U.S. interests, perhaps other U.S. business interests, are put at risk?

For an ambassador and an embassy facing this question, there is no manual to turn to. The answer depends on judgments about the local situation and local personalities. If the embassy turns push to shove on a commercial issue, will the host government step back, or shove back? Who will make mischief, and how? What is the totality of U.S. interests and demands, and what are their relative weights? And if the United States has lots of leverage—as it does in much of the world—how should that leverage be used to ensure that U.S. benefits are maximized and leverage preserved?

Guidance from Washington may be a mixed blessing on these kinds of questions, or no blessing at all. Washington agencies respond to their domestic constituencies. They may not be as well positioned to weigh trade-offs among issues or interests, and they may not be familiar enough with the local scene to make sound judgments about local reactions to U.S. pressure. Every ambassador can tell a story about waiting weeks for instructions that turn out to be blandly useless or internally contradictory—"get tough but cause no offense."

We've seen in Chuck Ford's story (pages 59–60) that sometimes a softer line than Washington is pushing can solve a problem quickly at a technical level, without the acrimony and delay that accompany political disputes. But sometimes an embassy can look at the local scene and see opportunities for aggressive action where Washington might shy away.

Paraguay, a smuggler's paradise, is a case in point. For decades Paraguay's Ciudad del Este, wedged between Brazil and Argentina, has moved tax-free liquor and cigarettes, high-end electronics, even garments and toys and footwear and other contraband into these large and protected markets.

But in recent years Brazil and Argentina have been cutting tariffs, and free trade is fatal to smugglers. So Ciudad del Este has turned increasingly to trademark knock-offs and pirated intellectual property, not to mention trade in false identities, illegitimate passports and arms and explosives.

Trademark theft involves slapping false labels on mobile phones, clothing, sneakers, "Barbie dolls" and "G.I. Joes," and other branded goods. Piracy involves making unlicensed copies of video and audio recordings, computer software, video games and other copyright-protected products. The International Intellectual Property Alliance (IIPA) estimates that lost or diverted U.S. trade due to piracy in Paraguay exceeded $220 million in 2000. Trademark theft and copyright piracy together probably cost U.S. companies more than total revenues from U.S. exports to Paraguay, which were just $389 million in 2000.

Embassy economic and commercial attaché Richard Boly saw that export promotion in this country of five and a half million people, most of them subsistence farmers and half under the age of fourteen, would have less payoff for American business than a concerted effort to curb the theft of intellectual property rights (IPR). He met with representatives of industries hurt by IPR piracy, their lawyers and U.S. government and local officials to determine which actions would be most effective. Paraguayan laws were more or less satisfactory, he learned, but their enforcement was weak and the conviction rate for violators close to zero. As he relates, "this analysis led me to focus on the role of public prosecutors and judges."

Boly used the leverage of a few dollars in local program funds to secure support from the Business Software Alliance, a U.S. trade association, for a case-study-based seminar that was offered to judges and prosecutors to help them learn how Paraguayan copyright law could be applied to software piracy. He also went face-to-face with members of Paraguay's Supreme Court on the judiciary's dismal record on IPR enforcement. When one justice challenged him to explain how bad-faith judges manipulated legal loopholes to protect the copyright pirates, he did the research and supplied the answers—and the justice repeated Boly's research in lectures of his own to magistrates around the country.

When Paraguayan police near the border arrested a high-profile IPR pirate with ties to Middle Eastern terrorists, a conviction seemed the least likely disposition of the case. The defendant's attorney was passing bribes to the judge and the prosecutor at the courthouse. Boly persuaded the presiding judge of the Supreme Court and the attorney general to intervene and have the prisoner transferred from a jail at the border to the national penitentiary in the capital. In an unrelated case, he got a Supreme Court justice to remove a corrupt judge who was ready to return a factory making pirated CDs to the crook from whom it had been seized. And he pressed yet another judge to cancel a planned sale of Nike's trademark rights, purportedly to cover an unpaid debt that a local attorney claimed the company owed him.

In most parts of the world, diplomats don't lean on judges. Ambassadors and their embassies are representatives of one sovereign to another, and in general they deal with executive-branch officials. Before telling a judge how to dispose of a case, most foreign diplomats in the United States would think twice—and then decide not to.

The invisible fence that keeps diplomats away from judges is a high barrier in Washington. If Boly had relied on Washington to send instructions, instead of taking action and giving Washington a chance to object, he might still be sitting at his desk in Asunción, waiting for the phone to ring. But Boly knew the local scene. He knew that the careful, methodical and fundamentally educational approach that P&G and the embassy used in China would likely fail in Paraguay's more personalized and much less disciplined environment. He did not buy into the prevailing view of Paraguay as a lost cause, and he had the energy and nerve for some radical action.

Commercial diplomacy sometimes demands the kind of aggressive intervention that Boly displayed in Paraguay. Commerce cannot thrive unless strangers can do business with each other, and that requires a rule of law. Support from the United States for an administration of justice based on law, precedent and fair dealing helps honest jurists assert the power of their offices against corruption and deceit.

In this case, the hard push brought big gains. According to IIPA testimony, trade losses due to violations of intellectual property rights, which had risen steadily from $10 million in 1993 to almost $300 million in 1999, dropped by 26 percent in 2000, the year after the embassy engaged the justice system on the issue. In 2001 Richard Boly received the Cobb Award (see page 6) for his gutsy performance.

SECTION 301

Trade agreements are tough to negotiate but even tougher to enforce. One reason why Richard Boly prevailed in Paraguay was the veiled but serious threat of legal action that could lead to trade sanctions. That threat hinges on the nature of trade agreements and on private-sector rights under U.S. law.

Codification of international rules on intellectual property rights and many other subjects—government procurement, investment promotion, rights of establishment and the like—have gravitated over the past twenty years toward trade agreements and toward the World Trade Organization. That is because trade agreements and the WTO have done a better job than other international agreements and organizations of solving the problem of enforcement.

Contrary to the lurid imagery of the antiglobalists, there are no Trade Police in blue helmets or black helicopters to swoop down upon offenders. But trade agreements are enforceable through the balance of concessions, one of the pillars of the original 1947 GATT and still an essential part of the world trading system.

Every party to a trade agreement, so the theory goes, makes concessions from which other parties benefit. The concessions may deal with market access, like a ceiling on a tariff or a floor under a quota, or with procedure, like a commitment to review antidumping orders every five years or to use only internationally accepted methods of testing imported beef for disease.

Each country that signs on to an agreement acknowledges thereby that the concessions are balanced, that in other words it got as good as it gave. If a party to an agreement later withdraws or fails to maintain a concession, the balance is said to be disturbed. To restore the balance, the party withdrawing the concession may offer new concessions in its place (compensation), or the parties that are injured by the withdrawal may withdraw concessions of their own (retaliation).

Enforcement of trade agreements has long been a preoccupation of the U.S. Congress, which under the U.S. Constitution is the branch of government responsible for foreign trade. Thirty years ago, in the Trade Act of 1974, the Congress gave the executive branch authority to retaliate (that is, to raise tariffs, impose quotas or take certain other punitive measures) when other countries engage in trade practices that violate international agreements or the international legal rights of the United States or restrict U.S. commerce in a discriminatory or unreasonable way. Further, Congress gave private parties—firms, trade associations, labor unions or any other "interested party"—the right to petition USTR to investigate specific foreign polices or practices and to act against them if warranted. The petition process gave the private sector a level of engagement and control over commercial diplomacy that was startling at the time but has been widely copied since.

These provisions, commonly called "Section 301," were expanded in later years to include special attention to protection and enforcement of intellectual property rights (IPR). Trade-policy insiders call the IPR provisions "Special 301."[8]

Special 301 requires the U.S. Trade Representative to identify to Congress by April 30 of each year countries that do not adequately protect U.S. intellectual property rights or that deny fair market access to U.S. persons that rely on intellectual property protection. Although the law requires a listing only of "priority" countries (that is, countries with egregious behavior and/or large adverse economic effect), USTR as a matter of practice also reports a "priority watch list," a "watch list," and a "special mention" category to cover comprehensively policies and practices that are prejudicial to U.S. intellectual property but may not rise to the "priority" level. Priority countries and practices face formal investigations that may result in retaliation. Countries on lesser lists face continued U.S. government scrutiny and a kind of public shaming that may make them less attractive to investors who depend on returns from patents, copyrights or trademarks.

Paraguay was identified as a priority country in January 1998 and signed a memorandum of understanding with the United States on protection of intellectual property later that year. Richard Boly's work with the country's judiciary took place within that context.[9]

The U.S. Trade Representative's office relies on U.S. intellectual property industries to furnish the information it needs for the compilation of the various lists that the law requires. Each year, the USTR places a notice in the Federal Register soliciting advice from the public with regard to which countries, acts, policies and practices should be targeted.[10] Responses to that notice tend toward the elaborate. The various copyright industries of the International Intellectual Property Alliance, file a read-only compact disc. PhRMA, the association that represents Pharmaceutical Research and Manufacturers of America, supplements its electronic filing with a loose-leaf binder that can be easily kept up to date. The PhRMA submission of February 12, 2004, provides information on intellectual property protection and market access issues in thirty-eight countries.

PhRMA's Susan Kling Finston calls Special 301 an excellent example of how embassies support American's most competitive business. The legal pressure of the Special 301 process, the diplomatic pressure and persuasion of the embassies, and the educational efforts of the industry come together in the early part of each year. After embassies get copies of PhRMA's submission to USTR, she says, they check the facts and comment from their perspective and the perspective of the host country. The embassies explain the issues in the local context and can plot a strategy for effecting change. They know who is a potential ally—perhaps a medical association that wants access to the latest therapeutic innovations or a company or university with potentially valuable research of its own—and what arguments will be most persuasive in the local political situation. And they have the human contacts, the personal relationships that are essential to building understanding.

With embassy advice, the industry knows how best to make its case, and with the threat of a formal U.S. government investigation and possible sanctions, the host government feels compelled to respond.

"Almost every year, there's an outstanding issue that gets resolved because of embassy intervention" using Special 301, says Finston. She cites the elimination of commercial piracy in the United Arab Emirates and the dramatic improvement in intellectual property protection in India as twenty-first century examples.

In the last few years the industry has mounted a strong effort to secure what it calls "data exclusivity." Finston explains that a pharmaceutical company that wants to bring a new product to market typically provides regulatory and licensing authorities, like the FDA in the United States, with a dossier containing the results of years of preclinical and clinical tests. A pharmaceutical manufacturer must invest on average $800 million to develop a new drug and most of that money is spent generating the data in the dossier. Yet some governments will release the data to companies that bore no share of the cost of producing it, or will allow a free-riding local manufacturer to claim "our drug is just like theirs, so you can use their data for our product." Without data exclusivity, says PhRMA, companies lose the incentive to develop new products, and untested and unsafe drugs may reach supposedly regulated markets.

The industry's approach to protecting data exclusivity involved first of all enlisting the full support of the U.S. government, in particular USTR. After all, unless and until the Trade Representative's Office signs on to the idea that a policy or practice is, in the language of the statute, "unjustifiable, unreasonable or discriminatory," private parties like PhRMA and its members won't get far complaining to foreign governments. PhRMA's appeal to USTR rested on the very solid ground of the WTO's 1994 Agreement on Trade Related Aspects of Intellectual Property Rights (Trips), which most of the WTO's 146 members have accepted. The Trips agreement requires that "test data submitted to governments in order to obtain marketing approval for new pharmaceutical or agricultural chemicals must ... be protected against unfair commercial use."[11]

While USTR pursued multilateral diplomacy at the World Trade Organization in Geneva, PhRMA turned to U.S. embassies to guide its work in key capitals. The results so far have been impressive.

- Almost all OECD-level countries (Poland and Turkey are exceptions) provide a minimum of five years of data exclusivity.[12]

- The American Embassy in Dubai used PhRMA's threat to petition for trade retaliation under Section 301 to secure data exclusivity in the United Arab Emirates.

- Jordan, closely linked to the United States through a bilateral free trade agreement signed in 1996, adopted effective data protection.

- In Tel Aviv Ambassador Daniel Kurtzer, with strong support from Undersecretaries Alan Larson at State and Kenneth Juster at Commerce, has pressed the government of Israel to abandon its refusal to recognize data exclusivity. The embassy helped to bring in an ally in Israel's world-renowned Weizmann Institute of Science. A policy change could occur in 2004.

- India used to be named with Brazil and Argentina as the countries most resistant to protecting intellectual property in the pharmaceutical sector. But India's economic transformation has led to, and been fostered by, a still evolving shift in policy. With the embassy's help, PhRMA has found some political support from India's Association of Biotechnology-led Enterprises (ABLE), of which it is an affiliated member. Commerce Undersecretary Juster uses the Indo-U.S. High Technology Cooperation Group, which he helped establish in 2002, to keep data exclusivity and related issues before India's top officials. Legislation to strengthen patent protection is likely to come before the parliament in mid-2004.

PhRMA uses Section 301 the way Congress designed it, as a tool that lets the private sector shape commercial diplomacy to enforce the rights negotiated in international trade agreements. In crafting the law, Congress did not worry too much about the friction its use might create, but private sector interests like PhRMA are sensitive to the diplomatic problems Section 301 can engender. PhRMA uses 301 on a global scale but recognizes that politics is local. Change comes about when the balance of local interests, political and commercial, favors change, and when local legal and political processes permit it. Too much friction can tilt the balance in the wrong direction. PhRMA, like other private sector petitioners, counts on American embassies, with their understanding of the local scene and their relationships with local decision makers, to make the case for change with as much efficiency and as little friction as possible.

Physical property: expropriation in Côte d'Ivoire

Sometimes energy and persistence and an iron-clad case are not enough. When a government refuses to stand by its own agreements, when the local courts provide no opportunity for due process, all the tools of persuasion and advocacy may fail to do the job. So far in Côte d'Ivoire, local political considerations have outweighed the desire for foreign investment, the risk that trade benefits may be lost, and the chance that Ivorian relations with the United States may deteriorate across a broad range of issues.

In 1995, the government of Côte d'Ivoire awarded temporary licenses to three cellular operators who pledged to build wireless communications networks in the country within twelve months. At the end of the twelve months, the government was to review the infrastructure and issue permanent licenses.

One of the licensees was Cora de Comstar SA, incorporated in Côte d'Ivoire but owned by an American company, International Wireless, and an Ivorian partner, Ibrahim Keita. In 1998, International Wireless, under its new name of Wireless Communications Technologies (WCT), negotiated the sale of 51 percent of its holding to an Ivorian named Alexandre Galley. But Galley never met the payment terms, and WCT asked the Commercial Court in Brussels to declare the agreement with Galley null and void.

In 1999, Western Wireless International and MAGIC (the Modern Africa Growth and Investment Company, an equity fund with backing from the U.S. government-owned Overseas Private Investment Corporation) bought out WCT and acquired 80 percent of Cora de Comstar for $30 million, indicating a valuation of $37.5 million for the entire company. The WWI-MAGIC group invested an additional $10 million to strengthen the network, which grew to forty thousand subscribers. The WWI-MAGIC investment followed extensive due diligence that confirmed that Cora held a long-term license and that WCT had clear title to its shares.

But as Riva Levinson of BKSH, a consultant to WWI-MAGIC, explains, "Sometimes even the best due diligence cannot guard against the uncertainties that occur when governments change, either though a political process or a military coup. Opposition politics is new to many parts of the world. So when regimes change, the newcomers often seek to change what their predecessors put in place. Investors can get caught in the middle when they find out they made business decisions based on a set of rules that no longer applies."

In late 1999 Côte d'Ivoire was sliding toward anarchy. On Christmas Day, a military coup overthrew the elected government. In late 2000, the leader of the new ruling junta, General Robert Guei, declared himself the winner of elections from which the main opposition leader had been excluded. The protests that greeted this fraudulent result were strong enough to cause Guei to step aside in favor of the runner-up, Laurent Gbagbo.

Since taking office Gbagbo has tried with very limited success to consolidate his power. A coup failed to oust him in September 2002, but he has not been able to suppress a rebellion in the Muslim north. In January 2003, under pressure from the French (who have several thousand peacekeeping troops in the country), he invited representatives of the rebels into the cabinet in a "unity government" which displays little unity and not much government. In March 2004 government forces fired on and killed scores of unarmed demonstrators in Abidjan while French forces reportedly stood by. Presidential elections scheduled for 2005 may not take place.

Cora de Comstar's struggle to protect its investment plays out against this backdrop of tumult and intrigue. In early 2001 the Gbagbo Government unilaterally changed the terms and conditions of its agreement with the cellular operators and set new fees payable at $51.2 million per license. The proposed fee, if enforced, would bankrupt Cora de Comstar and in fact, exceeded the valuation of the company.

Around the same time, Alexandre Galley resurfaced, claiming ownership of a controlling interest in Cora. Galley, it turned out, was a fugitive from justice in France, where under the name of Raphael Gnadre Dago he had been convicted and sentenced to twelve months in prison for counterfeiting. In addition, the United Nations Security Council named him in Resolution 1343 of June 4, 2001, which banned international travel for certain Liberian government officials and their close associates who were engaged in the illegal trade in arms and diamonds that fueled the civil wars in that country. Soon after President Gbagbo took office, Galley returned to Côte d'Ivoire and initiated legal action against Cora in local courts.

Galley lost repeatedly in the lower courts but won in the Ivorian Supreme Court. In May 2001, Ivorian police invaded the company's facilities and forced management and staff of Cora de Comstar to vacate the company offices. For the next two years the government of Côte d'Ivoire used its military and security services to support Galley, who was able to paralyze the business, threaten the personnel and win court orders to empty the company's bank accounts.

Cora's shareholders were left holding a very nasty bag. Their sunk investment was over $40 million. The retroactive license fee of over $50 million made the assets worthless. And Galley made operations impossible. At first, the shareholders of Cora tried to negotiate solutions to both problems directly with the government, believing that a negotiated commercial solution must be possible. The government had stated repeatedly that it sought and wanted U.S. investment, and with about 16 million in U.S. taxpayer dollars at stake through OPIC guarantees to MAGIC's investment, it seemed unlikely that Côte d'Ivoire would force MAGIC out. But compromise was not apparent. The U.S. shareholders initiated an advocacy effort in Washington to support their principled position. Letters were written, phone calls were made, programs were held up, but still the government of Côte d'Ivoire remained unwilling to address the enormous burden of the retroactive fee and Mr. Galley remained at large and able to use the authority and powers of the state—its security forces and courts—to undermine the U.S. company.

Arlene Render arrived in Côte d'Ivoire and presented her credentials as American ambassador in early 2002. Ambassador Render understood the importance of a commercially sustainable solution for the U.S. shareholders and hoped to put together a compromise acceptable to all parties.

With the support of the president of OPIC, the U.S. side proposed to the Côte d'Ivoire government that the license fee be paid over time, with revenues from the business, with certain benchmarks in subscriber growth that would trigger fees. While the shareholders preferred to pay no fees, and did not feel they were legally bound to, it was clear that the government would never accept such a position.

The government countered, agreed to consider such a payment plan, but then hardened its position. The ambassador, understanding that no other payment plan could be sustained, intervened on behalf of the shareholders and an agreement was eventually reached.

The problem of Mr. Galley proved more intractable. The shareholders, who continued to insist that Galley's claims had no basis in law, nevertheless proposed a settlement of Galley's claims. Ambassador Render and the embassy tried to mediate between the shareholders and the Ivorian government.

The Ivorian government in the end signed an agreement, but Galley continued to manipulate the courts, and government forces were used to enforce Galley's claims over the government's own agreement. The government's unwillingness or inability (perhaps some of each) to prevent the corruption of the courts left the shareholders with no redress.

As this drama played out, Cora de Comstar could not operate. No investor would put in equity and no lender would advance funds. The shareholders and the embassy abandoned efforts to find a settlement and placed the issue more clearly on a political basis.

Ambassador Render told the Ivorian government that the situation with Galley and Cora de Comstar raised basic questions about foreign investment and due process that put U.S. programmatic support for Côte d'Ivoire at risk. In the face of the ambassador's persistent pressure, the Gbagbo government agreed to sign a memorandum of understanding on the Galley issue.

But the MOU was never implemented. The government did not have the political will to rein in Galley nor the desire to shut down the network of corruption of which he was a part. On October 9, 2003 Galley again invaded Cora with the full support of Ivorian military police. He carted away the safes and held the employees at gunpoint. He controlled the facility for nine days, forcing the network to shut down and the destruction of the entire investment and its future potential earnings.

The shareholders have now asked the U.S. government to find that the government of Côte d'Ivoire expropriated their property, by failing to provide a minimum level of protection to the investment and by using its security forces in support of Galley's depredations.

The charge could trigger punitive actions. The Helms amendment to the Foreign Assistance Act requires the United States to oppose and vote against loans by international financial institutions like the World Bank to governments that expropriate American property without compensation. And U.S. trade preferences extended to Côte d'Ivoire under the African Growth and Opportunity Act, the Generalized System of Preferences and other legislation are also subject to withdrawal. These threats should strengthen the diplomats' hand.

Bribery: a global approach

The depth of corruption and criminality seen in Côte d'Ivoire is rare, though certainly not unique. Much more widespread is the subtle corruption of commerce through bribery, where often the provider of the bribe is an eager conspirator with the bribe-taker. The consumer, the public and honest competitors are the losers.

Until quite recently, international trade rules had nothing to say about bribery. The 1947 General Agreement on Tariffs and Trade established rules that governed the way a country could regulate or restrict trade at its borders, and it created elaborate procedures for multilateral negotiations to reduce those border measures. But on bribery it was silent.

There is no question that in countries where payment of bribes (more usually and politely called commissions), was a necessary part of business, U.S. firms were at a disadvantage. In the 1960s and 1970s, many U.S. companies decided that winning contracts mattered more than following the strictures of American business morality. Moral laxness produced scandal, and scandal led to legislation.

The Foreign Corrupt Practices Act (FCPA), enacted in 1977, places criminal penalties on American companies and individuals who make corrupt payments to foreign officials to win or hang on to business. Passage of the FCPA followed investigations by Congressional committees and by the executive branch that revealed that hundreds of U.S. firms looking for business abroad had made large payoffs, sometimes to win favorable decisions and sometimes just to get officials to carry out their duties.

The central idea of the FCPA is that bribery is as corrupting for the payer as for the payee. Nearly all Americans accepted the idea, but many foreigners did not. France, Germany and several other European countries, for example, treated bribes to foreign government officials as legitimate and tax-deductible business expenses. Soon after enactment of the FCPA, Congress felt a twinge of buyer's remorse: Did the legislation hobble U.S. firms in competition with foreign companies?

To its credit, Congress stuck with the antibribery statute, and in 1988 it directed the president to negotiate international antibribery agreements that would bring other countries up to FCPA standards. The drive to globalize the FCPA is commercial diplomacy on a multilateral plane, conducted not only by the Departments of State and Commerce, but the Treasury Department, the Department of Justice, the White House Office of Government Ethics and American multinational corporations.

Ambassador Mike Skol, one of America's leading anticorruption activists, says that the effort to build a worldwide consensus on a moral standard is the kind of diplomacy that often leads to criticism of the United States as "arrogant" and "intrusive." But as Skol points out, countries have come to recognize the soundness of the U.S. approach.

The American-led multilateral effort produced the OECD Convention on Combating the Bribery of Foreign Public Officials in International Business Practices (thirty-five members), which in effect internationalized the antibribery provisions of the FCPA. By 1999, the OECD member countries had introduced conforming laws and regulations to criminalize the payment of bribes and end their tax-deductibility.

The OECD convention, like the FCPA, was a supply-side effort that failed to address the solicitation or acceptance of bribes. Subsequent diplomatic efforts corrected that failing and produced the Inter-American Convention against Corruption (twenty-nine members), the African Union Convention on Preventing and Combating Corruption (twenty-one signatories), and most recently the comprehensive United Nations Convention against Corruption (signed by ninety-nine countries in December 2003).

Do these agreements work? The U.S. chapter of Transparency International (TI), the leading private sector, nongovernmental organization dedicated to combating corruption, agrees that success is hard to measure but sees signs of progress. In the twenty-six years since the FCPA was enacted, fifteen cases have been prosecuted in the United States. Since the conclusion of the OECD convention, there have been a handful of prosecutions in Europe and one in Canada. Most strikingly, says TI, legislation enacted in Nicaragua during the presidency of Roberto Aleman to bring that country into conformity with the Inter-American Convention against Corruption was used by the successor government to prosecute, convict and imprison Aleman himself on corruption charges. TI also points to the mutual legal assistance provisions of international anticorruption agreements that enabled the United States in January 2004 to return to Peru some $20 million embezzled by the government of former President Alberto Fujimori and deposited in U.S. banks. The same provisions may yet facilitate Fujimori's extradition to Peru from Japan.

The U.S. drive to internationalize anticorruption efforts has led to revisions in procurement and lending standards in the World Bank and the African, Asian, Inter-American and European development banks. The *Financial Times* agrees. "The change in attitudes toward bribery ... has come about largely as a result of U.S. diplomatic pressure."[13] And beyond agreements among government, U.S. private sector codes have been widely copied. Skol says that "the ethics code of General Electric, for example, is considered by many to be the global private sector standard."[14]

But for all this success with conventions, codes and standards, competition with firms that offer bribes, payoffs, commissions, kickbacks, sweeteners, inducements, baksheesh, blat or the like remains a major challenge for American companies and for American commercial diplomacy. According to the State Department, from early 1994 through early 2001 the U.S. government learned of significant allegations of bribery by foreign firms in over 400 competitions for international contracts valued at $200 billion. "The practice is global in scope, with firms from over fifty countries implicated in offering bribes for contracts in over 100 buyer countries during the seven-year period."[15] As a result, a number of companies are now pressing to have anticorruption clauses included in trade agreements.

"Trade agreements contain enforcement mechanisms," explains Diane Kohn of TI's U.S. chapter. "That's why advocates for issues like environmental protection and worker's rights gravitate toward trade negotiations." Multinationals and other U.S. businesses seeking a level playing field deserve credit for pushing transparency as a trade issue, and the U.S. government deserves credit for rising to the challenge. "NAFTA [North American Free Trade Agreement] had good transparency requirements for government procurement," Kohn says. "The government procurement section of the U.S.-Chile FTA went further, adding an antibribery clause. Then the Central American FTA [initialed in January 2004] applied the antibribery clause to all public officials involved with trade, not just procurement officers." The Central American agreement is now a starting point for bilateral free trade agreements under negotiation.

RAYTHEON IN BRAZIL

Because bribery is in most places a criminal act, most incidents that rise to the level of public awareness are either gaudy trials or unconfirmed rumors from unidentified sources. The famous story of the contest between the U.S. firm Raytheon and France's Thomson-CSF to win the contract for the SIVAM project in Brazil is a rare exception. The bribery in this case remains alleged, not proven. And the payoff—if ever offered—was never made.

SIVAM, for Sistema de Vigilância da Amazônia, or Amazon Surveillance System, was the billion-dollar plan of the Brazilian government to secure the vast and thinly populated Amazon region in the north and west of the country. Brasilia's control over the area, as large as the United States between the Rockies and the Appalachian Mountains, was spotty and uncertain. The central government had little ability to control illegal or unwanted activity—drug cultivation, processing and trafficking; illegal border crossings; unlicensed and untaxed gold mining by freelance prospectors, the poor and lawless garimpeiros; illegal felling and export of tropical hardwoods; encroachment by ranchers on land officially reserved for native tribes; ranching and farming, based on clearing the land with the illegal fires that environmentalists, especially in North America and Europe, deplored. Many Brazilians believed that if the Amazon were not brought more firmly under government control, the United States or the United

Nations or other international organizations would seek to assert authority over the region's resources.

Brazil's military was especially sensitive to potential challenges to Brazilian sovereignty in the Amazon. During twenty-one years of military rule (1964–1985), the government had spent heavily on road-building and riverine transport to encourage settlement in the region.

The military engineered a peaceful transition to civilian rule in 1985 but retained important influence over issues defined as "strategic," including regional development in the Amazon. And the army carried responsibility for defending the border. Military strategists developed plans in the late 1980s for a technologically sophisticated surveillance system that would allow Brasilia, with a minimum of manpower, to monitor events across this vast and poorly charted territory. The army's commitment to improved surveillance was sealed in 1991, when an incursion by Colombian guerrillas left three Brazilian soldiers dead and twelve wounded at a remote outpost.

Peter Wittkoff, in a thesis for the Naval Postgraduate School, describes SIVAM as a "technologically advanced command, control, coordination, communications, intelligence, surveillance and reconnaissance" system, based on "an integrated aggregation of sensors and radars" dispersed around the region and sending a constant data stream.[16] The data produced would serve multiple purposes, of which the most important were promoting ecologically sustainable development, curbing illegal activities, and securing the border. The cost of the system as designed was budgeted at close to $1.5 billion, a huge expenditure for a Brazilian government with limited resources. After several false starts and much internal struggle, Brazil's president approved the funding in 1993.

The project was mired in controversy from the beginning. President Itamar Franco, an elected vice president who assumed the presidency when his predecessor resigned to escape impeachment on corruption charges, decided early on that national security argued against an open and transparent bidding procedure. Instead, he established by decree a special multiagency commission to examine bids in confidence and ensure that the winning bid was competitive in price and technology. His purpose was to keep the project's specifications secret, but, as always, the side effect of secrecy was suspicion.

Sixty companies responded to the initial bidding documents, which the Brazilian government had circulated through foreign embassies. By April 1994, however, only seven bids were still under consideration, and three of those were rejected for failing to include financial plans. Two of the four remaining (the U.S. firm Unisys and a German-Italian group headed by Germany's Dasa) were eliminated on price. By the end of April, only France's Thomson and America's Raytheon were still in the running.

Washington pushed very hard for Raytheon. In January 1994, before the first bids had been submitted, Secretary of Commerce Ron Brown wrote to Brazil's Secretary of Strategic Affairs "in support of U.S. industry" generally. Once Raytheon became the sole U.S. contender, government support became stronger.

Without mentioning Raytheon by name, President Clinton wrote to President Franco in June, saying, "the U.S. government has provided a competitive financial package," a reference to Eximbank loans and guarantees in support of the export of the radar system that was the largest component of the contract.

The financial package was indeed competitive: It was an attractive alternative to the French package that Crédit Lyonnais had assembled with French government support, arguably in violation of the international Agreement on Export Credits, to which France, the United States and other members of the Organization for European Cooperation and Development all subscribed.[17]

President Clinton also held out the promise that "selection of U.S. firms could create opportunities for cooperation in environmental monitoring and protection, air traffic control and counternarcotics efforts." A more detailed letter from Commerce Secretary Ron Brown listed areas of cooperation between Brazil and several U.S. government agencies, including the National Oceanic and Atmospheric Administration (NOAA), NASA, the Forest Service, the Geological Survey, the Environmental Protection Agency, and the Federal Aviation Administration. The heads of NOAA and NASA sent letters as well. Perhaps most powerful, Ron Brown visited Brazil in June and made his pitch for Raytheon to President Franco personally, to other Brazilian officials and to the Brazilian press.

The intensity of the U.S. government effort depended partly on the size of the contract, but the desire to construct new ties to Brazil may have been equally important. U.S. relations during much of the twenty years of military rule in Brazil had been strained. In the 1970s, the United States had criticized Brazil's performance on human rights and had tried to block the government's nuclear ambitions. In the debt crisis of the 1980s, Brazil infuriated U.S. policy makers by seeking U.S. financial support while piling up barriers to U.S. trade and investment. So the opportunity in the 1990s to engage a U.S. firm, with U.S. government-backed financing, in a long-term, big-ticket project with Brazil's civilian government and professional army seemed a way to break with the past and broaden the base on which to build the relationship in the future.

High-level government attention backed up superior financing and superior technology that apparently gave Raytheon the edge. Thomson's bid called on the Brazilian government to issue new securities to finance the project, which Brazil was most reluctant to do. Raytheon, however, guaranteed full financing. Thomson's proposal advocated using over-the-horizon (OTH) radar for air traffic control; Raytheon argued, convincingly, that OTH radar was not sufficiently reliable or accurate for this task.[18] On July 18 the Brazilian government announced that Raytheon had been chosen the prime contractor on the SIVAM project. In December, Brazil's Congress authorized $1.35 billion in funding.

But the declaration of Raytheon as the winner was not the end of the game. Domestic and international scandal put the contract back into play in 1995. The CIA, it turned out, had given the Brazilian government evidence that Thomson had offered bribes to members of Brazil's armed forces. Peter Wittkoff writes:

> The U.S. and French press divulged in February 1995 that the U.S. Central Intelligence Agency reported in 1994 that Thomson CSF was paying bribes to win the SIVAM contract. French diplomats in turn accused the United States of bribing officials with $30 million. The French government proceeded to charge the United States with industrial espionage and unfair dealings The French claimed that CIA's information helped Raytheon win the contract. The Brazilian press received anonymous allegations that Raytheon had also paid bribes for the contract.... France expelled five staff members from the U.S. embassy in Paris.[19]

In an unrelated incident, a Brazilian software firm that was a Raytheon subcontractor was taken off the project in early 1995 after having been found guilty of tax fraud. Gilberto Miranda, a senator from the state of Amazonas who had opposed the original deal, argued that any switch in the subcontractors would require a new congressional vote. In late 1995, the Brazilian press obtained and published transcripts of secretly recorded conversations of presidential aides about SIVAM. One transcript recorded a senior aide to President Fernando Henrique

Cardoso (inaugurated January 1, 1995) asking a Raytheon representative if he knows "how much" Senator Miranda wants to drop his opposition. Another transcript indicated that an air force general who headed the Ministry of Aeronautics had spent two days at the home of a Raytheon's Brazilian representative. The revelation of the tapes led to the resignation of the air minister and of a cabinet officer widely believed to have been the source of the leak.[20]

The U.S. embassy, which had been quietly lobbying the Brazilian Congress throughout the bidding process, became less quiet as the possibility grew that the Raytheon selection might be overturned. Ambassador Mel Levitsky told the Brazilian press that an unjustified cancellation of the Raytheon deal could affect bilateral relations,[21] a remark that drew criticism from Brazilian political figures and commentators but that may have had an impact on later events. Officials at the Commerce Department and in the Export-Import Bank maintained their support for Raytheon.

The Brazilian Senate established a select committee to investigate the various scandals and allegations. In the end, the committee concluded that there was no evidence to implicate Raytheon or Senator Miranda in any illegal action. Brazil's Congress finally appropriated funds for SIVAM in 1997, and a court injunction against the project, related to the dismissal of the Brazilian software firm from the Raytheon consortium, was lifted at about the same time. The contract finally entered into force on July 25, 1997.

Secretary Brown later told the U.S. Congress that the SIVAM award to Raytheon was "proof of the indispensable role Commerce plays in assisting U.S. companies."[22] He might have added, the White House, NASA, the State Department and the Department of Defense.

And, of course, the Central Intelligence Agency. In a rare confirmation of CIA activity, James Woolsey, its director during the SIVAM affair, needled the complaining French in a *Wall Street Journal* opinion piece: "That's right, my continental friends, we have spied on you because you bribe. When we have caught you at it, you might be interested, we haven't said a word to the U.S. companies in the competition. Instead we go to the government you're bribing and tell its officials that we don't take kindly to such corruption.... This upsets you, and sometimes creates recriminations between your bribers and the other country's bribees, and this occasionally becomes a public scandal. We love it."[23]

VENEZUELAN NAVY

The threat of exposure that Woolsey employed to spectacular effect in Brazil works equally well on a smaller scale. Intelligence sources helped Mike Skol thwart a bribe and win a contract for an American shipbuilder in Venezuela, where Skol was ambassador from 1990 to 1993.

At that time, the Venezuelan navy put out a tender to refurbish six Italian-built destroyers that were showing their age. British, French and Italian companies entered the bidding, but to Skol's surprise no American firm sought the contract, which was worth upwards of a billion dollars. Without a U.S. company in the contest, some ambassadors might have moved on to other issues. But Skol knew something was wrong. He decided to poke around.

Skol asked Washington which American companies could undertake the work and learned that the Ingalls shipyard in Pascagoula, Mississippi was by far the most likely. Skol called Ingalls' CEO, who told him that the talk in the trade was of payoffs by the French and Italians to senior navy officers. Ingalls had no interest in fronting the cost of bidding in a rigged contest. Skol writes: "I asked him if Ingalls would consider joining the competition if I could guarantee the full support of the U.S. government, especially vis-à-vis the illicit activities of the Europeans. He said yes."

Skol gathered the information that U.S. intelligence and Ingalls' own sources could produce on the situation and went to President Carlos Andres Perez—CAP—with what was "not a threat (exactly)." CAP recognized the risks of exposure of the scandal and re-opened the tender, inviting Ingalls to compete. Skol later learned that CAP "told the Navy brass to stop," and eventually Ingalls won the bid.

COLOMBIAN AIR FORCE

The American embassy in Bogota used similar pressure to help a U.S. company overcome a sweetheart deal to sell French helicopters to the Colombian air force. President Belisario Betancur had come to Washington in 1985 to plead for helicopters to help fight the growing drug trade and the closely linked guerrilla insurgency. A U.S. defense department team, working with Colombia's air force, had surveyed Colombia's situation and had recommended a version of the Bell 212, which was already in the inventory of the national police and for which trained pilots and maintenance facilities were already available. The air force, which at the time relied on Bell helicopters almost exclusively, began to draw up specifications for a tender.

It was a galling surprise, therefore, when two years later commercial sources reported and the defense attaché confirmed that the Colombian air force was about to spend $36 million on Aerospatiale Puma helicopters, without notice or competitive bids. There were rumors of kickbacks and substantial sums passed under the table, but these were never proved. Ambassador Charles A. (Tony) Gillespie, Jr. called Washington and was reassured that an intervention on behalf of U.S. suppliers would be supported.

When confronted, the air force argued that the Bell 212 did not have the power and reach needed for the job. Gillespie raised the issue with the minister of defense, making all the arguments about maintenance and pilot training, the value of a transparent bidding process and the benefits of a solid relationship with the United States, from which the minister was then seeking assistance in other areas.

Gillespie was rebuffed—the minister insisted that the contract was signed, the deal done, the story over. Gillespie, however, persisted. For the next several weeks, the embassy's deputy chief of mission, the defense attaché, the head of the military group (the section of the embassy responsible for administering military assistance and training programs) and other embassy officers hammered away at their contacts in the air force and the ministry of defense, using the same arguments and asking that U.S. firms be given a chance. But the minister of defense continued to resist until Ambassador Gillespie indicated a willingness to go to the newly elected president, Virgilio Barco Vargas, who had a reputation for resistance to corruption. The defense minister then nullified the French contract "on technical grounds" and said he would welcome bids from U.S. firms, if they could meet delivery schedules already set with the French.

Bell Helicopter told the embassy that for its own reasons it would not compete for this sale. But just as Mike Skol did with Ingalls, Phil McLean, the State Department's director of Andean affairs, made a cold call to Sikorsky, whose UH-60 Blackhawk was undeniably superior to the Puma in power and reach. Sikorsky had been unaware of the opportunity but moved quickly to make room in its production schedule, so it could meet the timing the French had promised. The Department of Defense used funds available as foreign military assistance to facilitate financing arrangements.

Some months later, after Gillespie had moved on to another embassy, McLean joined President Barco at Palenquero air base to take delivery of five Sikorsky Blackhawks, the first of several dozen now deployed in Colombia in the war against terrorism and the narcotics trade.

▧ Commercial Diplomacy and the National Interest

MEXICO

High-level intervention and the spoken or unspoken threat of exposure also worked to inhibit unfair or corrupt practices in Mexico. Jim Jones, who served as ambassador to Mexico in 1993–1997, intervened to secure a re-bid on a government contract for oilfield services that was initially won by a French company that skirted the written rules. The more transparent re-bid went to a mid-size U.S. company. When local officials shook down a U.S. developer for an illegal payment in return for permits to build on land the developer owned west of Mexico City, Jones went to state and eventually federal officials "at the highest levels" to resolve the problem. And, says Jones, "as we did routinely in these kinds of issues, we also followed up with the company to make sure that retribution was not exacted against them in the future."

A change of administrations helped Ambassador Jeffrey Davidow (1998–2002) block a shady deal to sell French police radios in Mexico. The sale in question was part of a program of Mexico's central government to subsidize local purchases of standardized equipment, so that police agencies in different localities could communicate with each other. But the specifications published in the Official Gazette did not list standards of performance. To qualify for the subsidy, the local agency had to buy from a specific—in fact French—manufacturer.

Davidow protested to the newly elected government of Vicente Fox. "The new minister in charge of national security matters quickly understood what had happened," Davidow says. "He speculated that someone in the outgoing government had received a payoff from the French company or its Mexican distributors to write the specs as they were published. The minister wanted to help, but it took him and the embassy over six months of trench warfare to get the regulations re-written and the competition opened to the American company. In the end, we were successful, largely because the new cabinet minister did not have any desire to protect the special arrangements worked out by a different political party."

Sanctity of contracts

Theories of economic growth and development were transformed by events in the 1970s and 1980s. The calamitous impact of the oil price increases engineered by the producers' cartel in 1973 and 1979 led to the "lost decade" of the 1980s, when many developing economies contracted, living standards fell and poverty expanded. During that dark period, commercial banks and international financial institutions restructured many billions of dollars in unpayable debts owed by the developing world, and new lending to finance growth dried up.

During that period also, the idea that economic development required implanting indigenous industries across a wide range of sectors was discredited. Instead of this isolationist approach, which depended on government regulation and financial incentives to squeeze out imports and promote their replacement by locally produced merchandise, policy makers moved toward pro-market solutions that reduced the role of government in economic affairs. The set of closely related policies supporting pro-market development came to be known as the "Washington consensus." It included lower trade barriers, more competition, balanced budgets to take the state out of the capital markets, lower tax rates and lower subsidies, an end to fixed prices and overvalued currencies, deregulation, privatization and receptivity to foreign investment.

The U.S. government was a strong supporter of the consensus. Successive administrations broadly encouraged American firms to invest, and American banks to lend, where pro-market policies were being followed. Energy and telecommunications companies, many of them newly deregulated and able freely to deploy their capital around the world, were especially aggressive in responding.

In some cases, investors may have underestimated political risk. As one chastened energy executive said: "In this sector, it always gets back to politics. The minister of energy, the governor of the state, they want to appear to be helping the consumer by lowering prices. It may be contrary to contracts, treaties, laws, what have you, but the political imperative is, 'I'll deal with that later. First I have to win the election.'" When that happens, contracts are hard to enforce.

Under such circumstances, commercial diplomacy has limited room for maneuver. Can diplomacy offer something sufficiently appealing, or threaten something sufficiently appalling, to reverse a course of political mischief? And if so, is the reward worth the cost?

Here are two cases in which—so far, at least—commercial diplomacy has tried and failed to persuade a foreign government agency to fulfill its side of a contract with American energy companies.

INDIA

Sixty-three million people live in the southern state of Tamil Nadu, on the Bay of Bengal. It is a rapidly growing state that welcomes foreign investment in the high-technology services that have fueled much of

India's recent boom. But its government has made a power play in the power sector, and foreign investors are losing out.

The government of Tamil Nadu invited foreign companies to participate in the development of a privately owned power-generation industry that would supply the population's increasing demand for electricity. Five companies, four of them American, answered the call. Collectively they invested very nearly $1 billion in four power plants that together have the capacity to generate nearly 800 megawatts of electricity.

These foreign companies are competitors. Or would be, if there were a market worth competing for. Instead, the five firms find themselves working together to try to enforce their contracts with the state-run Tamil Nadu Electricity Board, which in a little over two years has run up arrearages of over $200 million and counting.

The Electricity Board, say the companies, has never met its obligations. Payments have typically run about 40 percent of what is owed, sometimes more, sometimes less, with supplemental payments to cover debt service. "It's just enough most months so that we can pay our workers, our fuel suppliers and the interest on our loans," said a representative of one of the foreign investors. "But no company has taken a dime out. There is no money for maintenance: if something breaks, it stays broken."

The board and the state do not dispute the validity of the contracts. On the contrary: When the companies complain, the state has responded with promises to pay that, in textbook passive-aggressive style, have been neither withdrawn nor fulfilled.

Or the state has proposed Catch-22 "solutions." Your price is too high, says the Electricity Board: you must reduce your costs and pass the savings through to us. The board helpfully suggested that the coal-fired plants switch to cheaper natural gas—while the state allocated all the available gas to other users. The Board also urged the companies to lower their costs by negotiating better rates from the Indian banks that financed the projects. But board payments have at times been so small that several of the companies are in technical default for failure to pay installments of principal, and banks do not typically offer better rates to customers in default.

The board is effectively controlled by the governor and chief minister of Tamil Nadu. Tamil Nadu is the only state in southern India that was part of the political coalition supporting the BJP party that governed in New Delhi from 1998 until May . Paradoxically, the party's desire to keep Tamil Nadu in the BJP alliance meant that the central government, which would have had limited influence over state-controlled utilities in the best of circumstances, may have had even less clout than usual. And as the companies learned when they sought help from the U.S. embassy and from agencies in Washington, U.S. influence and instruments of persuasion don't work very well at the state level.

"Every U.S. official, including [Deputy Secretary of State Richard] Armitage and [Undersecretary of the Treasury John] Taylor, has obtained a commitment from New Delhi that the utility board will sit down and talk with us and work out a schedule of payment," says a representative of one of the U.S. companies. "But it's been two years, and we have not had a single meeting."

The governor of Tamil Nadu has twice canceled meetings with the U.S. ambassador, as soon as she learned that he would raise the question of payments to the power companies. "The U.S. government has been very helpful," said a representative of one of the companies. "We've worked with the embassy, with State, Commerce and Treasury, even the National Security Council. They all have tried to get the point across to the Indians that if you want more foreign investment, you have to keep faith with foreign investors."

The options for the companies, and for the U.S. government, are few and unappealing. The companies have considered seeking international arbitration, which they are entitled to do under their contracts. "We've resisted the confrontational legal route because we thought we could find another way," says a company representative. "Frankly, the local courts would be a waste of time and money. International arbitration might produce a judgment in our favor, but then we would have to get the state to enforce it. And it isn't clear at all how we could do that."

The companies have no interest in asking the United States to cut off support for India in the World Bank and related financial institutions, as Cora de Comstar has done (pages 83–86). "We're all pretty tired of sanctions," a company representative said. "They don't work. Besides, we are trying to preserve our contract. We don't want to walk away from our investment with nothing."

But in an effort to build leverage, the companies lobbied in Washington for legislation that would address their case. Representative Robert Menendez (D-NJ) sponsored a bill that finds that "the Tamil Nadu Electricity Board has violated the principle of contract sanctity" and requires that none of the U.S. foreign assistance authorized by the FY 2004 appropriations act be used to "support any programs, projects or activities (other than humanitarian, health, or rule of law programs, projects, or activities) located in or designed to benefit the State of Tamil Nadu, India."

The Menendez amendment passed the House but was not included in the appropriations bill that was enacted into law in January 2004. Nevertheless, says a company representative, "if we can demonstrate that legislation on the Hill is not going away, that gets attention." There may be concern, in Tamil Nadu as well as in New Delhi, that if India loses support in the Congress, legislation to curb outsourcing will gather steam in Washington and in U.S. state capitals.

Some observers believe that the real motive of the Tamil Nadu state leadership is not populist electoral politics but cronyism. If the foreign investors can be forced to sell out for cents on the dollar, new buyers—friends of the governor?—can take over the plants with much lower fixed costs.

The situation in Tamil Nadu bears some resemblance to the much more widely known collapse of Enron's $2.8 billion investment in a 2,200 MW power project at Dabhol in the nearby state of Maharashtra. After four years of negotiations, the contract for that project was signed in 1995. In a climate of intense political controversy in India, the contract was renegotiated in 1996 to reduce the tariff and bring the state electricity board in as an equity partner.

Operations began in May 1999, but within a few months the state electricity board declared it could not pay the rates promised in the contract, and operations ceased in 2001.[24] According to an executive with an Enron successor company, U.S. commercial diplomacy on Enron's behalf was close to a breakthrough when the terrorist attacks of September 11, 2001, changed the order of priorities in U.S.-Indian relations. Then came the exposure of fraudulent accounting practices and Enron's collapse. The Dabhol plant now seems likely to be sold to local interests at a fraction of its cost.

The *Economist* magazine said Enron's long dispute with the state of Maharashtra could "do further harm to India's already blighted image as a destination for foreign direct investment."[25] But neither Enron's example nor the problems in Tamil Nadu seem to have had much effect on investment flows, and certainly not outside the power sector. Even in Tamil Nadu itself, there has been no drop-off in foreign investment. It may be that new investors are not aware of the situation in the power sector, which the companies have not been eager to publicize, especially to the Indian press. Or it may be that newcomers do not care. Investors in call centers or backroom processing or software development may believe that the behavior of the

Electricity Board and the governor and the chief minister has no relevance to their business.

One strong conclusion to draw from this is that commercial diplomacy has limited effectiveness at the state level. American ambassadors to India from Richard Celeste to Bob Blackwill to David Mulford have given strong support to U.S. investors, but their leverage, like their credentials, runs to the central government. Investors and diplomats should take note: political risk analysis must analyze the right set of politics.

A second conclusion is less obvious and more disheartening: a bad investment climate doesn't necessarily deter new investors. High-tech service investment continues to flow into Tamil Nadu, even while the governor stiffs the power companies. Competition, and the confidence of business leaders that they can outperform their colleagues, can drive investment into rising risk for long periods of time. Once foreign investors have committed their money, politicians may not feel much pressure from the market to treat the investors fairly, or well.

ARGENTINA

Risks and costs rise when rules are uncertain or unevenly applied. That proposition has rarely had a more dramatic or conclusive proof than during the crash of the peso in Argentina at the end of 2001.

The crash was more than a financial event. Other countries have moved from fixed-rate to floating-rate currencies with less political havoc and economic carnage. But Argentina not only revoked its irrevocable "Law of Convertibility" that tied the peso to the dollar. The government in sweeping decrees, sometime with and sometimes without the assent of the legislature, rewrote agreements between debtors and creditors, sellers and buyers, landlords and tenants, and workers and employers— without the consent of either side.

In a few short weeks, Argentina's currency lost 80 percent of its value. In a few short months, Argentina's GDP fell from $269 billion to $93 billion. One-third of the population was pushed below the poverty line. The country had five presidents in six months.

Scores of American investors sought their government's help in salvaging what they could. The U.S. government faced the crisis with multiple objectives: contain the crisis and prevent a spreading financial panic, ensure stability in the U.S. banking system, resist public assumption of private sector risk and the creation of "moral hazard," ensure fair treatment for American investors, promote democracy and the rule of law in Argentina and protect U.S. foreign policy options throughout the region for the long term. These objectives were not always compatible, and trade-offs are always difficult.

At least some U.S. investors with physical assets in Argentina look back on the crisis and conclude that U.S. commercial diplomacy let them down, perhaps through timidity, perhaps because other issues demanded available time and attention, or perhaps because the situation simply would not yield. For some, the failure of commercial diplomacy meant a slide into litigation.

Argentina's financial crisis had developed over a long period of time. In 1991, Argentina adopted a "Law of Convertibility" that fixed the rate of exchange of the peso at one-to-one with the U.S. dollar. The central bank was obliged to buy and sell pesos for $1.00 each. The fixed rate was intended to limit inflation, which had destroyed the country's savings in the 1980s, by preventing the government from printing money without dollars to back it up.

By the year 2000, however, the system was badly strained. Inflation had indeed been broken, but the government had been running persistently large budgetary deficits that were increasingly hard to finance. As the government's debts mounted, lenders' doubts about creditworthiness grew, and interest rates began to rise. The country slid into a vicious circle of rising debt and deteriorating ability to pay. Argentines as well as foreigners suspected that the "irrevocable" Law of Convertibility would have to be revoked. In 2001 wealthy Argentines in particular began moving their bank accounts offshore, and collapse seemed unavoidable. *The Wall Street Journal* called the growing crisis "the world's slowest train wreck."[26] In December 2001 the government abandoned the one-to-one exchange rate, and by late January the peso was worth about two bits.

Abandoning the convertibility law led Argentina's government and Congress to abandon just about every other kind of economic agreement. Banks were required to convert dollar-denominated loans into pesos at one rate of exchange, and dollar-denominated deposits at another. Banks depositors found their accounts first frozen, then partially thawed. Farmers who needed credit could not borrow, but farmers who had borrowed could pay off their "pesified" debts at twenty-five cents on the dollar. Three privatized sectors, energy, telecommunications and water, were forced to sell into the local market at prices fixed in pesos, though they were all financed by loans and bonds that had to be paid in dollars. And bondholders faced the largest sovereign default in history, about $135 billion.

One U.S. energy company that had entered the market during the privatization wave of the 1990s had seen the crash prefigured in Argentine behavior in 2000–2001. The company operated a gas-transportation system that supplied electricity to customers at a price fixed by contract in pesos, with an escalator clause tied to the U.S. rate of inflation measured by the producer price index (PPI). When the PPI rose, the company expected that approval of a corresponding price increase would be a formality. But Argentina's "ministro publico," a government official who acts as an advocate for consumers, sought and obtained a judge's injunction blocking the rate hike. The increase would be unfair, it was said, because there was no inflation in Argentina.

Then came the crash. In January 2002 Argentina adopted legislation to void all contracts denominated in dollars or in pesos linked to hard currency indices like the PPI. Electricity rates charged in pesos were frozen. With the company's costs (especially finance costs) still denominated in dollars, cash flow became deeply negative and the value of equity fell to near zero.

The company, in desperate condition, mobilized other firms in the sector and pleaded with Argentine authorities for relief. They were brushed off, a company executive said, with the line "you guys have been gouging us for years." Yet since privatization Argentina's energy prices had been the lowest in the region and among the lowest in the world.

According to the company, the U.S. government was sympathetic but of limited practical assistance. Before the crash, the embassy shied away from intervening, because it did not want to show a lack of confidence in Argentina's judicial system. After the crash U.S. policy makers, particularly in the Treasury Department, focused primarily on the financial crisis, not on its effect on direct investors. The embassy in Buenos Aires followed Washington's lead. "The embassy," a second U.S. energy company confirmed, "said its chief objective was preserving the democratic structure of Argentina's government. They didn't want another Venezuela. They couldn't or wouldn't engage. We got more support from the IMF and the World Bank than we did from the U.S. government."

A third U.S. company, a long-time investor in Argentina, was not concerned about Washington's approach. "We stayed in touch with the embassy, but mostly to listen," an executive said. "We carried our own water. We figured our contacts were better than theirs, and maybe our relations as well."

Some U.S. government officials see things differently. The assistant secretary of state for economic and business affairs, Tony Wayne, notes that after the crash he and Under Secretary Alan Larson began a series of monthly conference calls with the embassy in Buenos Aires and members of the American business community. The U.S. government, in its first contacts with the Argentine government that took office in May 2003, urged Argentina to open a dialogue with the American business community. U.S. Ambassador Lino Gutierrez, who arrived at his post in September 2003, invited government ministers and representatives of different business sectors to come together, in an effort to push that dialogue along. There have been some successes, but the process is difficult.

The government in Washington, like others, had seen the crash coming. As an embassy officer relates, while Argentines were moving their money out, the Federal Reserve was shipping dollars in—as much as $30 billion in currency in 2001, by some estimates. And the United States fully supported IMF loans to Argentina of $22 billion over the course of 2001. But the United States, which has the largest share of votes on the IMF board (17 percent), never demanded that the Fund make enforcement of contracts or other solutions to commercial problems a condition of its loan agreements. As far as the companies or the embassy were aware, the U.S. representatives at the IMF insisted only that Argentina adopt "a credible economic plan that is fair to American investors," without defining either "credible" or "fair."

After the crash, even more than before, leverage with Argentina is with the IMF. Some U.S. companies have begun to lobby the Fund directly, in hopes of securing conditions in the next loan agreement with Argentina that will address their concerns. Fund officials cannot be pleased.

For some American companies, the Argentine crisis was a notable failure in commercial diplomacy. Said one executive: "Our conclusion is that when an issue is as complicated as this one, with contracts and courts involved, the reception that business gets in the U.S. government is not enthusiastic. Maybe we failed to make the government understand what was happening, or maybe they had reasons for their passivity that they did not share with us." A U.S. diplomat on the scene disagrees but allows that financial issues had priority over commercial matters.

And companies have begun to litigate. About ten or a dozen companies whose contracts have been nullified are in or preparing to seek international arbitration, a right they are guaranteed by the U.S.-Argentina bilateral investment treaty (BIT). Argentina has asked the United States to agree that the right of access to arbitration does not extend to minority shareholders, which the U.S. investors are in most instances. The treaty requires that the two sides enter into consultation when either side requests it, and those consultations are underway. In the view of one U.S. company with a stake in the outcome, Argentina is "clearly trying to change the rules and mitigate its obligations under the BIT. If the United States succumbs," says a company representative, "it will make the protection the BIT affords meaningless."

Even if the United States does not succumb, U.S. investors face a long period of uncertainty. The consultations will take time to play out before arbitration can begin, and arbitration if it does begin will be a slow process at best. The problem of the nullified contracts could hang over U.S.-Argentine commercial relations for years to come.

Security

This book began with the assertion that the two great goals of American foreign policy are security and prosperity. These goals normally reinforce each other: a prosperous America can be more secure, and a secure America can be more prosperous. But exceptionally, in the interest of security, the government may adopt policies that interfere with commerce and the pursuit of prosperity. Commercial diplomacy then tries to minimize the damage.

Sanctions and export controls

The United States is by far the world leader in the application of economic sanctions to achieve political and security objectives. In a few cases, energetic diplomacy has successfully persuaded other countries to join in. In many more cases, diplomacy has failed to win multilateral support, and the United States has gone on to apply sanctions unilaterally.

MULTILATERAL SANCTIONS

Multilateral sanctions have enjoyed notable if limited success. During the Cold War, for example, U.S. diplomats negotiated an elaborate system to prevent the transfer to communist countries of goods or technologies with military applications. All the NATO countries (except Iceland) and Japan and Australia took part in a seventeen-member Coordinating Committee (CoCom) that developed lists of controlled items and procedures for licensing and tracking their trade and end use. Decisions required unanimity. At least in principle, no member country could license the export of a controlled item to a proscribed destination if any other member country objected. The system was balky but enjoyed broad support in the business community because it was multilateral. Companies from one country did not enjoy an advantage over their competitors elsewhere. And though there were more than a few serious breakdowns in which militarily significant items found their way to proscribed destinations, most observers credit CoCom with imposing heavy costs on the communist bloc and retarding the growth of its military power.

Since the Cold War, multilateral controls have eroded. CoCom has been replaced by overlapping arrangements aimed at preventing proliferation of nuclear, chemical and biological weapons of mass destruction and their delivery systems, as well as a number of conventional weapons systems. Many of the communist states that had been targets of the CoCom controls are now participants in multilateral export-control arrangements. But there is no central licensing system and there are deep disagreements among the participants about what goods and technologies need to be controlled and which destinations should be off limits. Strong opposition from the United States and others, for example, has not deterred Russia, a member of the Nuclear Suppliers Group, from continuing to supply nuclear equipment and technology to Iran.

Enforcement can be a problem. The United States may license "dual use" equipment—machinery that may be used in civilian or military production—for sale to a civilian end-user for a peaceful end use. The same commercial officers normally charged with promoting U.S. exports monitor the sanctions through plant visits, making sure that licensed goods are where they are supposed to be, doing what they are supposed to do. The two roles, promotor and enforcer, call for different kinds of expertise and can be difficult to combine.

Despite these failings, the logic of multilateral controls over trade in advanced weaponry and related technology is so compelling that virtually no voice of opposition is heard in the U.S. business community.

UNILATERAL SANCTIONS: BUSINESS GOES TO THE HILL

But there are other sanctions that enjoy much less favor. Unilateral sanctions, especially those that involve export controls, seem only to transfer business from the United States to third countries, imposing no significant burdens on the target of the sanctions and providing no incentive for changes in policies or behaviors. The use of such measures expanded dramatically after the Cold War. At the end of 1997, according to the Congressional Research Service, legislative statutes in force contained 191 sanctions-related provisions.[1] The president's Export Council counted seventy-three countries affected by U.S. unilateral sanctions in January 1997.[2] The cost to the United States by one estimate was $19 billion a year in exports, 250,000 jobs and $1 billion in national income.[3]

A number of export-oriented businesses formed a coalition called "USA*Engage" to oppose the spread of sanctions. Bill Lane, the director of the Washington office of Caterpillar, Inc., developed the lobbying group's strategy and served as its chairman.

▦ Commercial Diplomacy and the National Interest

Lane calls unilateral sanctions "foreign policy on the cheap." He says, "we sanctioned Colombia because of lack of transparency in their elections, we went after U.S. companies selling products to central China because of the Three Gorges Dam, we sanctioned South Korea and Saudi Arabia over labor rights, and India and Pakistan for nuclear testing." Under the Helms-Burton Act and the Iran-Libya Sanctions Act (ILSA), says Lane, we threatened extraterritorial action against companies and citizens in Mexico, Canada, the European Union, Israel and elsewhere that do business in Cuba or invest in Iran or help Libya develop its oil industry.[4] According to USA*Engage, in 1996 the United States imposed twenty-three unilateral sanctions, and "by 1997 over half the world's population was the target of some form of economic punishment."

"That was the high-water mark," Lane says. "In late 1996 business was ready to take the issue on. CEOs were ready. They travel the world. They know that if we threaten to sanction Egypt because of lack of religious freedom, it's a one-day, one-paragraph story in the Washington Post, but it's the top story in Cairo for days on end. If you're selling a product or a project that requires support and engagement for a long period of time, just the possibility of sanctions introduces an element of uncertainty that makes buyers nervous and that competitors exploit."

Lane began to assemble a lobbying coalition of companies affected by unilateral sanctions. "We thought we would get maybe 100 companies and a modest amount of money. We got 622 companies, and we were able to mount a strong effort in Washington and in the home districts of members of Congress."

Congressional support for the USA*Engage coalition followed quickly, and it was bipartisan. The foreign affairs committees supplied the most vocal friends of the coalition: Richard Lugar, then the second Republican (after chairman Jesse Helms) on the Senate Foreign Relations Committee, and Lee Hamilton, the ranking Democrat on the House International Relations Committee. Senators Chuck Hagel (R-NE) and Chris Dodd (D-CT) and representatives Don Manzullo (R-IL) and Phil Crane (R-IL) were also supporters.

Lane got universities and think-tanks involved, producing studies of sanctions, their costs and their effectiveness. "In studies, the score was something like 32-2 in favor of our point of view," Lane says. "We gave the Clinton administration good political cover."

The administration also seemed ready for a change. In its first term, the administration had tried to influence China's treatment of political dissidents by threatening drastic restrictions on Chinese access to the

U.S. market through denial of normal trade relations. But China ignored or rebuffed the threats, and the administration backed down.

That humiliation would not be repeated. In January 1998 Stu Eizenstat, then undersecretary of state for economic, business and agricultural affairs, set up a team to evaluate sanctions policy and "ensure that sanctions are part of a coherent strategy." Eizenstat's group concluded that trade sanctions work best when they are multilateral and are part of a much wider set of actions—a conclusion that the business community could easily endorse.

But the momentum achieved by the antisanctions lobby and its administration supporters in 1997 proved hard to sustain. USA*Engage and like-minded groups, including the National Foreign Trade Council, the U.S. Chamber of Commerce, the Small Business Exporters Association, the American Farm Bureau Federation and the National Association of Manufacturers, bought a full page of the January 16, 1998 edition of the *Wall Street Journal* to print an "Open Letter on Cuba." The letter cited the impending visit of Pope John Paul II to Cuba and called for an end to the embargo on exports of food and medicine. Bill Lane expected a rising tide of pro-engagement sentiment during the pope's five-day visit.

No such luck. On January 17, the day after the *Wall Street Journal* ad, lawyers for Paula Jones deposed President Clinton and asked about his relationship with Monica Lewinsky. On January 21, the day of the pope's arrival in Havana, Clinton told interviewers that he had never had an improper relationship with the intern and had never asked her to lie about it. The news had room for no other story. Network anchors left Cuba before sundown. The pontiff's historic visit became a media afterthought. The sanctions issue, like so many others, languished.

But events would not allow the United States its collective distraction for long. In May 1998, India and Pakistan detonated nuclear devices, and war that could kill millions suddenly seemed possible.

The crisis in south Asia made economic sanctions a first-tier issue. Under the Symington-Glenn (1976) and Glenn (1994) amendments to the Arms Export Control Act, the president was required to end most foreign assistance, military sales and government-backed financing programs for Pakistan and India, as well as to withhold U.S. support for new lending by the World Bank and other international financial institutions. The prospect of mandatory sanctions against two countries in which the United States needed to marshal every element of influence led to the passage in 1998 and 1999 of bills providing the president partial authority to waive the Symington and Glenn sanctions. "Model" sanctions legislation supported by USA*Engage attracted 185 co-sponsors in the House and came within five votes of passage in the Senate.

The congressional debate brought sanctions policy to broad public attention. Then, to the surprise and delight of USA*Engage, the national college debate tournament for 1999–2000 picked the topic, "RESOLVED: That the United States Federal Government should adopt a policy of constructive engagement, including the immediate removal of all or nearly all economic sanctions, with the government(s) of one or more of the following nation-states: Cuba, Iran, Iraq, Syria, North Korea." The number of hits on the coalition's website spiked. USA*Engage hurried to make sure its website covered both sides of the issue, so that debate-team members would not have to go elsewhere for their research. "We got a whole generation" of future leaders, says Lane.

Ten days after the attacks of September 11, 2001, the president waived nearly all sanctions against Pakistan and India. Except for Cuba, and a few exceptions like Syria, the sanctions debate is pretty well over, at least for now. "No one talks any more about conducting foreign policy on the cheap," says Lane.

The use of commercial diplomacy to advance security has turned toward homeland defense.

Securing the borders

The openness of America's border was a source of pride before September 11. After the attacks, it became a source of concern, even of fear. Before September 11, foreigners enjoyed easy access to the United States and nearly unchecked freedom once admitted.[5] That would end. Imports arriving at U.S. ports were brought across the border in a paperwork operation aimed at speed and efficiency and largely disconnected from the physical goods themselves. That too would change.

With the creation of the Department of Homeland Security (DHS), first established as the Office of Homeland Security in October 2001, and elevated to a cabinet-level department in January 2003, the many agencies engaged in different aspects of border control were brought under a single command. For trade and travel, the Customs Service and the border-control functions of the Immigration and Naturalization Service and the Animal and Plant Health Inspection Service were placed in a 40,000-man Bureau of Customs and Border Protection (CBP) in the DHS Directorate of Border and Transportation Security.

The consular service, which issues visas to foreign travelers, remained in the Department of State. But Section 428 of the Homeland Security Act of 2002 assigned to DHS the authority to administer and enforce the immigration laws, including laws relating to the function of consular officers in issuing or denying visas. Under a memorandum of understanding that the two departments signed in September 2003, the Department of State manages the visa process and Homeland Security sets visa policy.

To strengthen security for both goods and people, DHS developed a model called "smart borders." The goal is to identify the areas of greatest risk, concentrate resources in those areas, and push the border outward, away from the homeland. "Smart borders" implies using technology to improve inspection of cargoes and travelers, and using diplomacy to persuade foreign countries, businesses and individuals to cooperate.

Along with the Department of State, agencies of the Department of Homeland Security directed and often carried out much of the diplomatic work. As of this writing, there has been much more success in dealing with traded goods than with travel and travelers.

GOODS

Over 90 percent of the world's traded goods travel in seaborne containers. Seven million cargo containers arrived at U.S. seaports in 2002, carrying nearly half of the country's $1.2 trillion in imported goods. Reducing the risk of that trade is the aim of the Container Security Initiative (CSI), a program involving tighter regulation, improved technology and diplomatic implementation.

Tighter regulation includes the 24-hour rule, promulgated by DHS, which requires that CBP be provided with information about cargoes destined for the United States 24 hours before the cargoes are loaded in foreign ports. Improved technology includes vehicle and cargo inspection systems (VACIS) with radiation-detection equipment and scanners that can penetrate steel for nonintrusive inspection of containers, and secure seals that will readily show evidence of tampering. Diplomatic implementation includes sending CBP teams to foreign ports to work with local customs services and port authorities.

The container security initiative imposes costs on foreign countries. The United States does not defray the initial or operating costs of high-tech screening systems. And the CSI is just one of an alphabet soup of measures and programs to improve the security of international freight by protecting the supply chain from the point of production to the U.S. border:

- C-TPAT the Customs-Trade Partnership against Terrorism, is a voluntary program in which importers, customs brokers, carriers and foreign manufacturers who comply with and enforce security standards established by Customs and Border Protection, in turn receive expedited processing (more precisely, reduced likelihood of inspection) of their cargoes.

- FAST (Free and Secure Trade) expedites truck transport between the United States and Canada, and the United States and Mexico, for cargoes that are C-TPAT compliant. If the carrier, the importers and others that figure in the supply chain are C-TPAT compliant, and the driver has been vetted and carries a FAST identification card, then the cargo can move in a dedicated traffic lane at the border through a paperless inspection that relies on bar-code scanning technology.

- ACE (Automated Commercial Environment), a planned secure, "single screen" internet-based data system that the international business community can use to interact with all U.S. government agencies on import/export requirements, and that the agencies can use to interact with each other. The ACE will improve access to supply-chain data needed to anticipate, identify, track and intercept high-risk shipments. DHS also plans to link the ACE to biometric identification systems.[6]

- It has no acronym, but the Bioterrorism Act, administered jointly by the Food and Drug Administration and Customs and Border Protection, requires foreign suppliers of food products to maintain records that will allow any shipment to be traced all the way back to the farm or ranch or fishery, and to appoint agents in the United States responsible for keeping the FDA informed in advance of shipments.

In the early stages of the CSI and related measures, there was considerable foreign resistance to what some saw as another unilateral U.S. response to terrorism, or another example of the extraterritorial reach of U.S. policy. Cris Arcos, DHS director of international affairs and a former U.S. ambassador to Honduras, explains that American officials took a number of steps to counter this attitude:

- Multilateralism: The CSI was negotiated bilaterally with the most important ports (twenty ports in fifteen countries account for over two-thirds of all cargo containers entering U.S. seaports), but the United States promoted the initiative in the Group of Eight, the World Customs Organization, the International Maritime Organization, and other international bodies. Port security standards developed multilaterally in the International Maritime Organization and the International Civil Aviation Organization were integrated into and made a prerequisite for the CSI.

- Reciprocity: Foreign customs and port officials were invited to visit U.S. ports to observe U.S. procedures in action.

- Efficiency: U.S. officials were able to demonstrate that nonintrusive inspection and sealing of containers could take place during the time that the containers would normally be in the port waiting to be loaded on vessels. At the U.S. end, however, containers that had been inspected and sealed abroad would clear customs without additional inspection, a net increase in efficiency.

- Equity: When foreign officials (especially in the European Union) complained that CSI-certified ports would take business from other ports, the United States agreed to accelerate negotiation of agreements with additional ports. Ports began to compete to embrace CSI, rather than band together to resist it.

- Technical assistance: The Department of State asked the Trade and Development Agency (see pages 51–52) to educate developing-country airports, seaports, railways and customs services about the need to secure the supply chain in order to remain competitive in the U.S. market. USTDA organized a demonstration project in the Asia-Pacific region and worked with DHS, the World Customs Organization and private firms such as Oracle, SAIC, Motorola and Savi Technology to mount a transportation security conference in Egypt in February 2004. That conference aimed primarily at bringing ports and customs services in Africa, South Asia and the Middle East into compliance with CSI standards, and not at all incidentally at linking U.S. suppliers of technology and equipment to procurement officers from around the region.

A key turning point in the drive to secure foreign cooperation was the demonstration that in addition to better security, increased attention to the supply chain provides commercial benefits for importers and traders. For example, it is not just Customs and Border Protection that receives news of shipments 24 hours before departure; importers and consignees also get the word. That leads to closer links between buyers and carriers, and carriers and exporters, with opportunities for improvements in efficiency all along the line.[7]

It helped as well that there was a sense of inevitability about the program. No country, port or carrier doubted that the United States had the need, the right, the ability and the determination to strengthen border security. Refusal to cooperate would be pointless and costly.

The State Department's assistant secretary for economic and business affairs, Tony Wayne, laid out the diplomatic strategy. "We had to make sure that everyone could see the initiative was aimed at security. Nobody wants to learn that a dangerous cargo came out of his port. And then when we were able to show concrete advantages to participation, to getting the seal of approval, people made a mental shift and saw the initiative as something positive, which could improve economic efficiency as well as security. Once they adopted this frame of mind, it became a lot easier to move forward and other ports started asking to join."

These diplomatic efforts have been successful. Programs to strengthen the security of the flow of goods across U.S. borders have been carried out, at least so far, with remarkably little friction or disruption to trade.

PEOPLE

Unfortunately, the alphabet soup of programs to tighten security in the flow of people across U.S. borders has proven much less palatable.[8] People are harder to handle than cargo. A container has a unique number and doesn't complain when it is fitted with a transponder or tagged with a bar code. People do not have unique names (there are haystacks of Wangs, Parks, Lals, Murads) and resist being tagged or tracked. Containers go where they are sent, people go where they want.

The United States now requires that foreign travelers from all but Canada and twenty-seven mostly European countries obtain visas, and that nearly all visa applicants be interviewed in person by an American consular officer.[9] Even though the number of visa applications has fallen from an annual rate of 10.5 million before September 11, 2001 to about 6.5 million in 2003, and even though the number of visa officers has risen from around 800 to close to 950, the interview workload is crushing. According to the State Department's Janice Jacobs, a deputy assistant secretary for consular affairs, at twenty of the busiest posts appointments must be scheduled four or five weeks in advance. Many applicants require additional security screening, adding unpredictable days or weeks to processing time. Nevertheless, as this book goes to press Assistant Secretary of State for Consular Affairs Maura Harty insists that additional resources are not required.

The interview workload could soar in October 2004, when by law nationals with new passports from the twenty-seven countries for which visas are now waived will have to get visas, unless their passports contain machine-readable biometric information, such as the digitized image of a fingerprint. As of this writing, only Australia and New Zealand are likely to be issuing passports that meet this standard by the statutory deadline. Even U.S. passports will not meet the standard by the due date.

And what the State Department's visa instructions for foreigners calls "the world's foremost security database" is not in the best of shape. The agencies that maintain lists of dangerous or suspect foreigners, principally the Departments of State and Justice (FBI) and the Central Intelligence Agency, still do not communicate easily with each other. Multiple queries and multiple searches are needed to scan the relevant files. The technical challenge of integration is heightened by privacy concerns. The currency of the data is questionable. The clearance process is time consuming, and many question its value. DHS officials say integration should be completed by the summer of 2004.

The government agencies involved are not yet working well together. Within DHS, the Bureau of Customs and Border Protection reports to the undersecretary for border and transportation security (Asa Hutchinson), and the Bureau of Citizenship and Immigration Services report to the deputy secretary. Coordination is imperfect. The September 2003 memorandum of understanding between the Departments of State and Homeland Security was the beginning of what could be a difficult reorganization, in which responsibility and accountability may become separated.

Implementation of tighter controls on foreigners seeking to enter or traveling inside the United States has had a large commercial impact, not just on travel and tourism but on hospitals and clinics with foreign patients, schools and universities with foreign students, and any company that operates across the border and needs to bring its foreign personnel, customers, suppliers and investors to these shores. The expectation that the adverse effect of new rules and procedures would be short lived has not been met.

Travel and tourism have been hit hard. The number of foreign visitors to the United States fell from 51 million in 2000 to 42 million in

2002. With an extra push from the weakening dollar, the travel and tourism surplus—the difference between what foreign visitors spend here and American travelers spend abroad—has dropped even more sharply, from $26 billion in 1996 to $3.9 billion in 2003.

Education has also suffered severely. Foreign applications to U.S. graduate schools are down by a third in 2004 over 2003, according to the Council of Graduate Schools. China and Muslim nations are most affected.[10]

The evidence of the harm that tighter visa problems have caused for commerce in general is largely anecdotal, but there is plenty of it. The Lebanese vice president of a U.S. company, employed in Beirut, held a simple U.S. business (B-1) visa for fifteen years. When his visa needed renewal, he applied five months before his expected travel date. He had to wait four months for an interview and three more months for approval and missed his meetings. A U.S. energy company has shifted the venue of negotiations with a Russian company to Russia, because the Russian negotiators cannot reliably obtain visas in a timely way. Buyers from a Sichuan factory needed ten weeks to get visas to inspect a $2.4 million machine they had agreed—in principle—to purchase. Venezuelan oil executives on a one-day buying mission to Houston spent four and half hours at the airport to clear entry procedures; they had no time left for business. Because of visa delays beyond the expected six weeks, a U.S. money-center bank could not bring the corporate officers of a foreign business partner to a presentation on an upcoming corporate bond offering.

Indian employees of U.S. companies have been unable to obtain visas for scheduled training. An Indonesian national who works for a U.S. company and is based in the United States returned to Indonesia on emergency travel and had to wait four months for an appointment for visa revalidation. A similar situation snagged an Egyptian employee, an executive intra-company transferee, for ten weeks in Egypt. while his family remained in Texas. Visa processing time for British intra-company transferees has increased from four to six days to four to six weeks. Beyond delays, U.S. businesses complain that visa requirements and decision making are arbitrary, varying from place to place and from month to month. The lack of predictability makes planning difficult or impossible and creates deep frustration for host and traveler alike.

The business consequences have been serious: lost opportunities; lost sales; cancellation or relocation of conferences, trade shows, and contract negotiations; a preference for outsourcing over U.S.-based training; a damaged reputation for reliability with foreign customers, suppliers and governments; production delays and increased costs; and a competitive advantage eagerly seized by U.S. competitors.

As with cargoes, the volume of traffic across the border is far too large to allow careful screening of all entries and exits. Jackie Bednarz of DHS says there are about 500 million border crossings per year, about half by American citizens. The business community, the State Department and DHS all arrive easily at the same conclusion: there needs to be a program for people comparable to C-TPAT for goods, a way to identify known "trusted travelers" so that screening resources can be concentrated on unknown and higher-risk applicants for entry. But the goal is elusive.

Government agencies also ask how far it is safe to trust business advice. One DHS official asks if businesses that vouch for a foreign visitor should be asked to post a bond. Another asks if businesses would cover the costs of an "express lane" at ports of entry and exit for trusted travelers. The answers are not entirely clear as this book goes to press, but business and government are grappling with the problems.

Two business efforts can be singled out. The Travel Business Roundtable and the U.S. Chamber of Commerce are working with DHS on ways to alleviate the impact of tighter visa procedures on tourism and the hospitality industry. And the Business Council for International Understanding (BCIU) has assembled a group of business representatives that meets frequently with senior officials from the Departments of State and Homeland Security to design a trusted-traveler program. BCIU is hopeful that its efforts will produce a visa process that is faster and more predictable, without compromising security.

Conclusion

This book could have had the subtitle: "How American Embassies Make Our Country Rich and Strong." We have focused on the Departments of Commerce and State, their programs and people. We have said very little about export finance, project finance, the Export-Import Bank or the Overseas Private Investment Corporation. We have only touched on the work of the U.S. Trade Representative, and we have ignored the important commercial diplomacy conducted by the Departments of Treasury, Defense, Energy, Justice and Labor. We have not discussed the excellent and successful export-promotion programs of the Department of Agriculture, whose cooperation with American farmers and food producers is in many ways a model that other agencies and sectors could emulate. A true review of U.S. commercial diplomacy would need to take into account all this activity and more. But even this truncated survey leads to some general conclusions.

The global success of American business means prosperity at home and influence abroad. The diplomatic effort needed to promote American business is, as we have seen, cheap, powerful and effective. Yet commercial diplomacy remains controversial. A sizable body of opinion opposes government support for U.S. exports and overseas investment as "corporate welfare." And some U.S. companies operating overseas make it their policy not to seek U.S. government assistance or advice, at least not until they get into serious trouble. These attitudes need to change.

The links between the U.S. economy and the rest of the world grow richer and more complex by the day. We saw earlier how rising energy costs caused foreign trade to double its relative weight in the U.S. economy in the decade of the 1970s. In the 1990s, falling costs for communications and transportation had a similar effect. Imports and exports of goods and services and earnings on foreign investments, which were about 25 percent of our gross national product at the beginning of the decade, are about 30 percent of our $11 trillion economy today. The same pattern can be seen in the balance sheets of our greatest corporations: a rising share of revenue comes from business overseas. And the federal government finances a rising share of its budget deficit by selling its securities to foreigners, who now hold about 40 percent of the federal debt.

Globalization of American business and the American economy is a fact of life, whether or not we like it. And like it we have. The United States has thrived as its global linkages have multiplied. In the 1990s per capita income measured by real purchasing power rose faster in the United States than in almost any other country in the world.[1]

Business success owes a great deal to United States foreign policy. As the Cold War came to an end, American leadership helped to forge a global consensus that favored a shift from government-directed to market-directed economic development, accompanied by liberalization of trade and investment flows, privatization, deregulation, protection of property rights, fiscal discipline and monetary stabilization.[2] The economic expansion that followed, including the amazing transformations now taking place in China and India, depended in large measure on the widespread acceptance of these ideas.

And U.S. foreign policy owes a great deal to business success. The example and undeniable attraction of American prosperity are the most persuasive arguments we have in support of our political goals around the world—the spread of the rule of law, the free flow of information and ideas, and individual freedom.

The risks in today's globalized economic environment are considerable and not wholly understood. In the developing countries that have engaged most aggressively with the United States and the world economy—China, India, Indonesia, Thailand, Korea, Mexico and others mentioned prominently in this book—economic reforms, social aspirations and political conflict seem to give impetus to each other, creating an accelerating and widening spiral of change that may not be sustainable or even manageable, and whose ultimate direction is not predictable.

Links run in all directions. Events in countries where U.S. business is peacefully and progressively engaged can have the most profound effects on U.S. security. Terrorism too has global reach. We need to do what we can to ensure that a country's openness to American ideas and ideals, and to American products and capital and business relationships, does not end in a backlash of turmoil and violence. The responsibility for success is not the government's alone. American companies are, in the words of former Undersecretary of Commerce Jeffrey Garten, "de facto agents of foreign policy."[3] U.S. business did not choose this role and may not want it but cannot escape it. It comes with the territory.

▨ Commercial Diplomacy and the National Interest

Recommendations

What can be done now to strengthen America's commercial diplomacy? First, a change of attitude. The executive branch and the Congress need to recognize that America's commercial power is the primary source of American global leadership, because it is our commercial power that other countries willingly follow. Protecting and expanding the U.S. role as the world's supplier and customer of choice for goods, services, ideas, capital and entrepreneurial energy should be a foreign policy objective second only to securing the homeland. The natural coalition supporting this idea is potentially large: business, labor, agriculture, finance and higher education will all benefit when protecting American commercial power moves to the top of our national priorities.

Second, adjustments in policy. Major changes may not be required, but pro-commerce policies need to be applied with greater urgency and vigor.

- We need to resolve the visa mess, not tomorrow but today. Visa delays, denials and black-hole procedures put American commercial leadership at risk. The intentions of the visa agencies have so far been better than their performance. Meanwhile, companies struggle with their foreign employees, customers and suppliers. The growing U.S. reputation for hostility to foreign visitors may cause the next generation of the world's leaders to look elsewhere for their education and for their models of political and economic organization. Every day's delay in fixing the visa problem is years of trouble down the road.

- We need to enforce our trade and investment agreements, and we must abide by them as well. That is no small order. USTR lists 274 agreements concluded between 1984 and 2003,[4] and many more are under negotiation. But without enforcement, what's the point? Perceived problems in enforcement leave many members of Congress with the suspicion that the United States is getting snookered in the trade bazaar. That is why they denied the president trade negotiating authority from 1995 until 2002, when they restored it by a single, skeptical vote. Enforcement of existing agreements, more than any other action, can win over the doubters in Congress. And U.S. adherence to its agreements is an obvious condition for foreign compliance. Commerce and USTR have recently increased their enforcement budgets: the investigative and legal resources are in place. Diplomats try to wall off trade disputes from other issues, but they cannot always succeed. Is the administration politically prepared for the international confrontations that enforcement inevitably brings?

- Global theft of intellectual property, on which so many American companies depend, continues to grow. We may need to devise new ways to monitor and enforce existing agreements, and to make new agreements more readily enforceable.

- We need to drain the ideology from export controls. As we have seen, unilateral sanctions are largely in the past. That is where they need to stay.

- We don't need to reorganize. The present commercial policy set-up may not be perfect, but there has been constant tweaking since 1980. A few years of stability could be beneficial.

These small policy moves are less important than the recognition of the real importance of commercial power. When our priorities are straight, good decisions will follow. When there is a consensus across party lines that America's commercial clout is a cause, not a by-product, of America's global influence, policies will fall in line, and the modest resources needed to conduct those policies will be provided. The Business Council for International Understanding and the American Academy of Diplomacy intend this book to move us toward that consensus and toward a more prosperous and secure America.

Appendix I

Bill of Rights for U.S. Business

American business has a right:

First, to have its views heard and considered on foreign policy issues that affect business interests;

Second, to be assured that the ground rules for the conduct of international trade are fair and nondiscriminatory;

Third, to receive assistance from well-trained and knowledgeable trade specialists in each overseas mission;

Fourth, to receive sound professional advice and analysis on the local political and business environment;

Fifth, to receive assistance in contacts with key public and private-sector decision makers;

Sixth, to the active promotion of U.S. firms in international bids, and where more than one U.S. firm is involved, even-handed support for all interested firms;

Seventh, to receive assistance in achieving amicable settlement of investment and trade disputes, and in cases of expropriation or similar action, to obtain prompt, adequate and effective compensation.

November 30, 1989

Appendix II

State Department FY 2005 International Affairs Summary

($ in millions)	FY 2003 Actual	FY 2004 Estimate	FY 2005 Request
INTERNATIONAL AFFAIRS	31,214	29,412	31,519
FOREIGN OPERATIONS	21,440	19,564	21,331
Export-Import Bank of the United States (net)	564	54	156
Overseas Private Investment Corporation (net)	(239)	(199)	(187)
Trade and Development Agency (TDA)	47	50	50
Child Survival & Health Programs Fund (CSH)	1,940	1,824	1,420
Global Fund to Fight AIDS, Tuberculosis, & Malaria	[248]	[398]	[100]
Development Assistance (DA)	1,480	1,377	1,329
International Disaster and Famine Assistance	432	474	386
Transition Initiatives	62	55	63
Development Credit Authority (DCA)	8	8	8
USAID Operating Expenses (OE)	593	641	623
USAID Capital Investment Fund	43	98	65
USAID Inspector General Operating Expenses (IG)	33	35	35
Economic Support Fund (ESF)	4,802	3,263	2,520
Assistance for Eastern Europe and the Baltic States (SEED)	522	442	410
Assistance for the Independent States of the FSU	755	584	550
Peace Corps	295	308	401
Inter-American Foundation	16	16	15
African Development Foundation	19	19	17
Millennium Challenge Corporation	-	994	2,500
International Narcotics Control and Law Enforcement (INCLE)	245	460	359
Andean Counterdrug Initiative (ACI)	842	727	731
Migration and Refugee Assistance (MRA)	782	756	730
U.S. Emergency Refugee & Migration Assistance (ERMA)	106	30	20
Nonproliferation, Anti-Terrorism, Demining (NADR)	332	396	415
Global HIV/AIDS Initiative	-	488	1,450
Treasury Technical Assistance	13	19	18
Debt Restructuring	-	94	200
U.S. Emergency Fund for Complex Foreign Crises	-	-	100
International Military Education & Training (IMET)	79	91	90
Foreign Military Financing (FMF)	5,992	4,633	4,958

($ in millions)	FY 2003 Actual	FY 2004 Estimate	FY 2005 Request
Peacekeeping Operations (PKO)	214	124	104
International Financial Institutions	1,296	1,383	1,493
Multilateral Development Banks Arrears	[65]	[97]	[59]
International Organizations & Programs (IO&P)	169	320	304
COMMERCE, JUSTICE, STATE	8,016	8,646	8,981
Diplomatic & Consular Programs	3,888	4,220	4,285
Capital Investment Fund	182	79	155
Embassy Security, Construction & Maintenance	1,405	1,421	1,539
Other State Programs	352	503	422
Contributions to International Organizations	894	1,000	1,194
Contributions for International Peacekeeping Activities	636	695	650
Related Appropriations (e.g., Asia Foundation,NED)	71	78	103
Broadcasting Board of Governors	534	592	569
International Trade Commission and Other Programs	55	59	63
AGRICULTURE -P.L. 480 Title II	1,741	1,185	1,185
LABOR, HHS -United States Institute of Peace	16	17	22
IRAQ RELIEF AND RECONSTRUCTION FUND (IRRF)	2,236	18,439	-
GRAND TOTAL, INTERNATIONAL AFFAIRS w/IRRF	33,450	47,851	31,519

General Notes:
- Detail in this table may not add to the totals due to rounding.
- Prior to 2004, the International Disaster and Famine Assistance account was called the International Disaster Assistance account.
- The FY 2003 Actual level reflects $168 million in rescissions and includes $5.8 billion in emergency supplemental appropriations for Iraq, Afghanistan and coalition allies, including reimbursements from the Iraq Relief and Reconstruction Fund. See table that follows.
- FY 2004 Estimate level reflects $198 million in rescissions and includes $2.7 billion in emergency supplemental appropriations for Iraq and Afghanistan, including mandatory transfers from the Iraq Relief and Reconstruction Fund and emergency response funds reprogrammed for acceleration of reconstruction in Afghanistan.

Notes

Chapter 1, *The Basics*, pages 1–15

1 The Commerce Department estimates that $1 billion in merchandise exports supports 22,000 jobs, and that jobs supported by exports pay 13 to 18 percent above the national average wage. The estimate was last revised in 2000.

2 Press release, U.S. Census Bureau, Department of Commerce, February 13, 2004.

3 Direct investment is the establishment of a new business or the acquisition of an existing business, as opposed to indirect or portfolio investment in bonds or small holdings of stocks. Direct investment is generally longer term and less liquid than indirect investment. The dollar values cited here were calculated by the Commerce Department's Bureau of Economic Analysis on a historical-cost basis, as of the end of 2002.

4 Commerce Department press release of March 12, 2004. These are preliminary figures, subject to revision.

5 A survey of the literature can be found at Lipsey, Robert E., *Home and Host Country Effects of FDI, Paper on ISIT Challenges to Globalization*, Lidingö, Sweden, May 24 to 25, 2002. See also Lipsey's paper, Foreign Production by U.S. Firms and Parent Firm Employment, NBER Working Paper No. w7357, Issued in September 1999. Lipsey's work is available from the National Bureau of Economic Research at http://papers.nber.org. The *Financial Times* reports that on the related issue of "offshoring," recent research has pointed out the benefits to the U.S. economy and to U.S. employment. Matthew Slaughter of the Amos Tuck School of Business at Dartmouth College says that "Expanding an overseas network frequently means you have to hire more workers in the US too." A study co-authored by Nobel laureate Lawrence Klein estimates that offshoring in the information technology sector will add 317,000 US jobs per year by 2008. See *Financial Times*, April 1, 2004.

6 The Foreign Trade and Investment Act of 1972, known as the Burke-Hartke bill, would have changed the tax treatment of foreign-earned corporate income so as to raise the effective rate on that income to 70–80 percent. The bill would also have empowered the president to prohibit overseas investment and the use of U.S. patents abroad in order to protect U.S. employment. On the trade side, Burke-Hartke would have restricted imports with quotas designed to hold the ratio of imports to domestic production for broad categories of goods to 1967–1969 levels.

7 U.S. Commerce Department data in 2000 chained dollars.

8 Section 207 of the Foreign Service Act of 1980 (Public Law 96-465, October 17, 1980, as amended).

9 At this writing John Wolf is the head of the U.S. Coordination and Monitoring Mission in Jerusalem (the president's special envoy for the Middle East peace process). He has served as assistant secretary of state for Nonproliferation Affairs, special adviser to the president and secretary of state for Caspian Basin Energy Diplomacy, ambassador for APEC (Asia-Pacific Economic Cooperation forum) and ambassador to Malaysia.

10 Executive Order 12870 of September 30, 1993.

11 The Trade Expansion Act of 1962 established USTR as the Office of the U.S. Special Trade Representative, changed to Office of the U.S. Trade Representative in the Trade Agreements Act of 1979.

12 The Trade Act of 1974 created the cabinet-level Trade Policy Committee under USTR's chairmanship. USTR subsequently used its own authority to establish the subcabinet Trade Policy Review Group and Trade Policy Staff Committee.

13 Section 207 of the Foreign Service Act of 1980 (Pub. L. 96-465, October 17, 1980, as amended)

14 The letter is published as Exhibit 013.2 to Chapter 013 of Volume 1 of the Foreign Affairs Manual (1 FAM 013 Exhibit 013.2). The Foreign Affairs Manual is available on the Department of State's Freedom of Information Act electronic reading room, http://foia.state.gov.

15 The $31.5 billion international affairs budget is the "150 account," so called after its accounting code number. The State Department itself accounts for less than $10 billion of the $31.5 billion requested. That pays salaries and expenses for 11,000 Foreign Service Officers, 9,500 foreign-national overseas employees and 7,500 civil service officers, and operating expenses for 261 embassies, consulates and other posts in 180 countries. It also funds embassy construction, security and maintenance; covers support for international organizations and conferences; and funds the Andean Antidrug Initiative and other programs. The remaining $22.5 billion in the 150 account funds all foreign aid and foreign military assistance; the Export-Import Bank, the Overseas Private Investment Corporation and the Trade and Development Agency; capital contributions to the International Monetary Fund, the World Bank, and the Asian, African, Inter-American and European Development Banks; and U.S. support for the United Nations and other international organizations. A summary of the FY 2005 request is attached at Appendix II p. 123.

16 The guidelines are posted on the website of the Commerce Department's Advocacy Center at http://export.gov/Advocacy/guidelines.html

17 Boeing, *Annual Report 2002*, p.11.

18 Letter from T. Allan McArtor, chairman of Airbus North American Holdings, December 11, 2003, posted at http://www.airbusnorthamerica.com/newsroom/letterfrom.asp.

Chapter 2, *Building a Strategy,* pages 16–37

1 Under a take-or-pay contract, the power-generation company agrees to produce, and the power-distribution company agrees to buy, a minimum amount of electricity, generally at a minimum price. So long as the producer meets its commitment to make the power available, the buyer is obliged to pay for it, even if the buyer does not actually take or consume the power. The take-or-pay contract places on the local utility—in this case the BPBD—most of the risk if demand for electricity falls short of projections.

2 Under the 1976 Arms Export Control Act, Congress must be notified of any proposed sale of "major defense equipment" valued at $14 million or more. If Congress fails to pass a joint resolution of disapproval within thirty days of notification (fifteen days for NATO countries, Australia, New Zealand and Japan), the sale may go through.

3 Indonesia, Malaysia, the Philippines, Singapore and Thailand founded ASEAN in 1967. The organization has since added Brunei, Burma, Cambodia, Laos and Vietnam.

4 John Monjo in Indonesia, Frank Wisner in the Philippines, David Lambertson in Thailand, Under Secretary for Economic Affairs Bob Zoellick, Deputy Secretary Larry Eagleburger.

5 The ten BEMs were Argentina, Brazil, China, India, Indonesia, Mexico, Poland, South Africa, South Korea and Turkey. Garten was undersecretary of commerce for international trade in 1993–1995.

6 Under the trade-mission program, the Department of Commerce organizes delegations of about a dozen companies, usually led by their CEOs or COOs, to visit a country or region and explore trade and investment opportunities with private sector leaders and government officials. The delegations are put together from companies in the same or closely related sectors and usually include both new-to-market and established firms. Participants cover their costs. Trade missions came through Thailand every month on average in 1996, and their sudden cessation in 1997 seemed to validate the Thai belief that U.S. business was around only in fat times, not in lean.

Chapter 3, *Market Access*, pages 39–68

1 Veteran trade negotiators will feel a kinship with Mark Twain's *Connecticut Yankee*, who received a near-fatal blow during "a misunderstanding conducted with crowbars."

2 Section 2101(a)(1), Trade Act of 2002.

3 The Export-Import Bank Act bars Exim from providing financing to Marxist-Leninist countries. President Clinton issued a national-interest waiver of this provision in April 1998, but Exim's first transaction in Vietnam came only in 2003.

4 U.S. International Trade in Goods and Services, Annual Revision 2001, Bureau of Economic Analysis, U.S. Department of Commerce, Washington DC, June 20, 2002, at http://www.bea.gov.

5 Presentation by Toby Bright, executive vice president for sales, Boeing Commercial Airplanes, Reston, VA, May 12, 2003.

6 Ibid.

7 Ibid.

8 Ibid.

9 A good account of this and other allegedly corrupt aircraft sales can be found in *The Economist*, June 16, 2003, pp. 55–58.

10 Canadian merged into Air Canada in 2000. Air Canada is now in bankruptcy reorganization.

11 *The Economist*, June 16, 2003, pp. 56.

12 "Those perfidious Anglo spies," *The Economist*, April 27, 2000.

13 OCP Ecuador SA, included Occidental Petroleum of the United States, which had a 12-percent stake. Other participants were Alberta Energy Company (Canada), Agip Petroleum (Italy), Kerr-McGee (USA), Repsol-YPF (Spain), Perez Companc (Argentina), and construction company Techint (Argentina).

14 When the fix is in, other tactics are called for. See pp. 75-78 [piracy in Paraguay].

15 The meeting in Austria followed "best practices" learned elsewhere. A similar meeting of pharmaceutical company representatives and interested ambassadors took place under AmCham auspices in Belgium in 2002.

16 Kazakhstan applied for WTO membership in January 1996. Its application is pending.

Chapter 4, *Rules,* pages 69–105

1 U.S. House of Representatives, Committee on Ways and Means, Overview and Compilation of U.S. Trade Statutes, 2003 Edition, Washington, DC, June 2003, pp. 504–622.

2 Thurow, Lester. *Fortune Favors the Bold: What We Must Do to Build a New and Lasting Prosperity.* New York: HarperCollins (2003), p. 170.

3 *Copyright Industries in the U.S. Economy: The 2002 Report,* International Intellectual Property Alliance, Washington, DC, pp. 21–22. The numbers refer to the output of the "core" copyright industries, defined by the IIPA as the motion picture industry (television, theatrical, and home video), the recording industry (records, tapes and CDs), the music publishing industry, the book, journal and newspaper publishing industry, the computer software industry (including data processing, business applications and interactive entertainment software on all platforms), legitimate theater, advertising, and the radio, television and cable broadcasting industries.

4 Ibid, p. 24.

5 Cited in "Counterfeiting and Theft of Tangible Intellectual Property: Challenges and Solutions," statement of Richard E. Willard, senior vice president and general counsel of The Gillette Company, before the Senate Judiciary Committee, March 23, 2004.

6 The Agreement on Trade-Related Aspects of Intellectual Property Rights, or TRIPS, is available on the website of the World Trade Organization at http://www.wto.org.

7 The similarity of approach has an explanation. Mars and Estée Lauder employed the same consultant, Marietta Bernot of International Trade Services Corporation.

8 Overview and Compilation of U.S. Trade Statutes, op. cit., pp. 119–131 and 622–647.

9 The U.S.-Paraguay MOU expired in 2003. It is now under renegotiation.

10 The most recent notice is at 69 FR 718, January 6, 2004.

11 See "Understanding the WTO: The Agreements: Intellectual property: protection and enforcement" on the WTO website at http://www.wto.org.

12 The Paris-based Organization for European Cooperation and Development (OECD) is a nontreaty group of thirty mostly high-income countries that traces its origins to implementation of the Marshall Plan after World War II. Many new issues in international trade are first debated in the OECD and are carried to the WTO or other broader forums only after an OECD-wide consensus is achieved.

13 Thomas Catan and Joshua Chaffin, "Comment and Analysis: Corruption," *Financial Times,* May 8, 2003.

14 The portion of General Electric's code of conduct that deals with bribery states: "GE employees should not offer anything of value to obtain any improper advantage in selling goods and services, conducting financial transactions or representing the company's interests to governmental authorities." Every GE employee must sign a pledge to abide by the full GE integrity policy, called "The Spirit and the Letter." The policy is posted on GE's website at http://www.ge.com/en/commitment/social/integrity/integrity.htm.

15 *Fighting Global Corruption: Business Risk Management,* Department of State Publication 10731, Washington, DC, May, 2001, p. 3.

16 E. Peter Wittkoff, "Amazon Surveillance System (SIVAM): U.S. and Brazilian Cooperation." Thesis, Naval Postgraduate School. Monterey, California: 1999, page xix. The thesis is available on the NPS website at http://library.nps.navy.mil.

17 Paul Cleveland (see p. 30) served on a Washington task force that analyzed the French export-credit proposal. He indicates that much of the U.S. information on the French proposal came from intelligence sources.

18 Wittkoff, op. cit., p. 27.

19 Ibid., p. 28.

20 Gabriel Escobar, "Casting Radar Net over Amazon Proves Touchy," *Washington Post*, December 4, 1995.

21 Wittkoff, p. 32.

22 Ibid., p. 33.

23 R. James Woolsey, *Wall Street Journal*, March 17, 2000.

24 For a good account of the Enron project, see: Choukroun, Sylvie. "Enron in Maharashtra: Power Sector Development and National Identity in Modern India." http://lauder.wharton.upenn.edu/home/pdf/Choukroun.pdf.

25 *The Economist*, April 19, 2001.

26 *Wall Street Journal*, July 16, 2001.

Chapter 5, *Security*, pages 106–117

1 Dianne E. Rennack and Robert D. Shuey, "Economic Sanctions to Achieve U.S. Foreign Policy Goals: Discussion and Guide to Current Law," CRS Report for Congress 97-949 F (Congressional Research Service, June 5, 1998).

2 "A Review of Existing Sanctions and Their Impacts on U.S. Economic Interests with Recommendations for Policy and Process Improvement". Submitted by the President's Export Council, Subcommittee on Export Administration (PECSEA) to the White House, June 1997.

3 Hufbauer, Gary Clyde, Jeffrey Schott and Kimberley Ann Elliott, "U.S. Economic Sanctions: Their Impact on Trade, Jobs, and Wages." Working paper. Washington, DC: Institute for International Economics, 1997.

4 Both ILSA and Helms-Burton give the president the authority to waive the extraterritorial application of U.S. law.

5 Foreigners residing here illegally were about 2.5 percent of the U.S. population in 2000, an estimated 7 million people in a population of 285 million, according to the Immigration and Naturalizatin Services (USCIS). See "Immigratin Statistics" as http://www.uscis.gov.

6 See http://www.customs.gov/xp/cgov/toolbox/about/modernization/ace

7 See "Importers pay the price of heavy security," *Financial Times*, January 13, 2004.

8 A partial list of acronyms and abbreviations includes:
  • CLASS: Consular Lookout and Support System. A State Department system used by consular officers to check names of all visa and passport applicants.
  • NSEERS: National Security Entry-Exit Registration System. A Justice Department system requiring the registration, of certain aliens, mostly males from Muslim countries. Replaced at the end of 2003 by US VISIT.
  • SAO: Security Advisory Opinion.
  • SEVISE: Student and Exchange Visitor Information System. Requires schools to track foreign students' name, address and enrollment status in a centralized database.
  • USA PATRIOT Act: United and Strengthening America by Providing Appropriate Tools Required to Intercept and Obstruct Terrorism Act of 2001.

- US VISIT: U.S. Visitor & Immigration Status Indication Technology System. A DHS system using digital photography and electronic fingerprint scanning to track entry and exit of foreign visitors with visas. In place now at top 50 ports of entry, full implementation planned by end 2005.
- Visas Condor: required security check covering all males aged six to forty-five from twenty-six mostly Middle Eastern countries.
- Visas Mantis: required security check for travelers studying or working in areas identified on the Technology Alert List.

9 At the discretion of the consular officer, interviews may be waived for persons under sixteen or over sixty; government officials and diplomats; persons seeking timely revalidation of their visas; and persons traveling on certain medical or other emergencies.

10 See *Wall Street Journal*, May 13, 2004, and *Financial Times*, May 13, 2004.

Conclusion, pages 118–121

1 World Bank, World Development Indicators, Gross National Income Per Capita at Purchasing Power Parity, available at http://www.worldbank.org. See also the World Economic Outlook Database, available on the website of the International Monetary Fund at http://www.imf.org. In 1992, the purchasing power of the average German's income was 89 percent of the average American's; by 2001 it had fallen to just 73 percent. The purchasing power of the average income in France fell from 83 to 72 percent of the U.S. level, and in Japan the drop was from 87 to 77 percent. Americans widened the prosperity gap with nearly every country except China, where purchasing power per capita rose from 6 percent to 9 percent of the U.S. level. Purchasing power parity calculations are intended to eliminate distortions created when differences in international exchange rates do not reflect differences in relative prices. At the PPP rate, one international dollar has the same purchasing power over domestic gross national income as the U.S. dollar has over U.S. gross national income. If changes in per capita income in the 1992–2001 decade were calculated at market exchange rates instead of at purchasing power parity, the apparent growth in the gap between incomes in the U.S. and in other countries would have been much larger.

2 John Williamson of the Institute for International Economics gets credit for coining the phrase "Washington consensus" in 1989.

3 Garten, Jeffrey E., "Business and Foreign Policy," *Foreign Affairs*, May/June 1997, p. 70.

4 U.S. Trade Representative, 2003 Annual Report of the President of the United States on the Trade Agreements Program, Washington DC, March 2004, Annex III. The count excludes agreements, such as textile quota agreements, that are monitored and enforced by other agencies.

Index

A

Abu Dhabi...17, 18, 19, 20, 22

ACE (Automated Commercial Environment)...112

Advocacy Center...6, 8, 12, 13, 19, 21, 126

ADWEA (Abu Dhabi Water and Electric Authority)...18, 19, 21, 22

AES (Applied Energy Systems)...17, 22, 23, 24, 25

Afghanistan...2, 52

African Growth and Opportunity Act...86

Agreement on Export Credits...91

Agreement on Trade in Civil Aircraft...54

Agreement on Trade Related Aspects of Intellectual Property Rights (TRIPS)...81

Agriculture, Department of...8, 118

Airbus...13, 14, 53, 54, 55, 56, 126

aircraft...2, 7, 14, 26, 27, 28, 29, 53, 54, 55, 56, 73, 127

Al Taweelah...17, 18, 19, 22

ambassador...5, 6, 7, 9, 10, 15, 17, 18, 19, 22, 23, 24, 26, 30, 32, 35, 36, 41, 42, 43, 44, 47, 50, 51, 54, 55, 58, 63, 65, 66, 67, 73, 75, 76, 82, 85, 87, 93, 94, 95, 96, 99, 104, 112, 125

Amerada Hess...15

American Academy of Diplomacy...121

American Chamber of Commerce (AmCham)...33, 35, 36, 63, 64, 65, 66, 67, 127

American Farm Bureau Federation...109

American International Group (AIG)...31

Amoco...15

AMRAAM...28

Anand, Panyarachun...36

Andean Antidrug Initiative...126

arbitration...99, 104, 105

Arco (Arco Oil and Gas)...15

Arcos, Cresencio (Cris)...112

Argentina...76, 82, 101, 102, 103, 104, 127

Armitage, Richard...99

Arms Export Control Act...109, 126

Asahi Glass...41

ASEAN Ambassadors Tour...31

ASEAN Free Trade Area (AFTA)...40, 49, 50

Asia Society...50

Asian Development Bank (ADB)...23

Association of Biotechnology-led Enterprises (ABLE)...82

Association of European Motorcycle Manufacturers...60, 61

Association of Southeast Asian Nations (Asean)...29, 30, 31, 32, 34, 40, 49, 126

Australia...35, 44, 106, 115, 126

Austria...62, 63, 64, 127

Automotive Industry Development Strategy...49

Azerbaijan...15

B

Babidge, Mark...44
Bachelet, Michell...29
BAE Systems...53
Baker, James...55
Baku-Tbilisi-Ceyhan...15, 45
Bangkok...32, 35, 36
Bangladesh...17, 22, 23, 24, 56
Bangladesh Power Development Board (BPDB)...24
Barco, Virgilio Vargas...95
Barry, Robert...75
Bechtel Corporation...15
Belgium...127
Belgrade...73
Bell Helicopter Textron (Bell)...94, 95
Benham, Liam...49
Bernot, Marietta...128
Betancur, Belisario...94
Bill of Rights for American Business...6
bioterrorism...9, 112
BKSH... 83
Black Sea...15
BMW...60, 61
Boeing...13, 14, 26, 27, 31, 53, 54, 55, 56, 126, 127
Boly, Richard...77, 78, 80
Bombardier...55
Bosporus Straits...15
Bowe, Peter...45, 47, 48, 54
Boyce, Skip...43
BP...15
Brandes, Jay...13
Brazil...31, 32, 38, 76, 82, 89, 90, 91, 92, 93, 127
bribery...56, 57, 86, 87, 88, 89, 128
Bright, Toby...127
Brown, Lyons Jr....63
Brown, Ron...6, 47, 91, 93
Brussels...9, 60, 83
Bucaram, Abdala...57
budget...9, 11, 12, 45, 46, 47, 51, 58, 68, 119, 126
Bureau of Customs and Border Protection (CBP)...110, 111, 112, 115
Bureau of Economic Analysis...125, 127
Burghardt, Ray...50, 51
Burke-Hartke bill...125
Bush administration...6, 28
Bush, George H.W....30, 55
Bush, George W....6, 10
Business Council for International Understanding...5, 31, 117, 121
Business Software Alliance...77

C

Canada...14, 45, 46, 54, 55, 88, 108, 112, 114, 127
Canadair...54, 55
Caspian...7, 15, 125

Caterpillar, Inc....107
Caucasus...7, 15
Central Asia...7, 31, 67
Central Intelligence Agency (CIA)...115
Chiang Mai...35
Chiang Rai...35
Chile...26, 27, 28, 29, 44, 89
China...14, 29, 31, 41, 56, 71, 72, 73, 74, 75, 78, 108, 109, 119, 127, 130
China Assocation of Enterprises with Foreign Investment (CAEFI)...73
Chirac, Jacques...55
chocolate — see also M&M chocolate candies...74
Cino, Maria...50
Clare, Gwen...58
Cleveland, Paul...30
Clinton administration...6, 28, 56, 108
Clinton, William Jefferson (Bill)...6, 25, 26, 27, 33, 37, 48, 56, 91, 109, 127
CMS Energy...17, 18, 19, 20, 21, 22
CNN (Cable News Network)...31
Cobb, Charles E. Jr....6
Coca-Cola...71
Cohen, William...27, 29, 36
Cold War...26, 106, 107, 119
Commerce, Department of...5, 10, 12, 13, 19, 30, 32, 45, 46, 53, 60, 61, 63, 93, 99,
    120, 125, 126, 127
Compania Telefonica de Chile...44
Congressional Research Service...107, 129
Container Security Initiative (CSI)...111, 112, 113
contracts...4, 12, 16, 22, 23, 24, 43, 44, 47, 55, 59, 68, 89, 91, 92, 93, 94, 95, 96, 97,
    99, 100, 103, 116, 126
Coordinating Committee (CoCom)...106, 107
Cora de Comstar...83, 84, 85, 86, 99
Côte d'Ivoire...82, 83, 84, 85, 86
Council of Economic Advisers...9
Crane, Edward...108
Cuba...59, 108, 109, 110
customs...33, 34, 40, 51, 59, 68, 70, 71, 110, 111, 112, 113, 114, 129

D
Daimler Chrysler...54
Daley...19, 21
Dartmouth College...125
Davidow, Jeffrey...96
Dayton Accords...52
Defense, Department of...8, 14, 93
Delta Airlines...31
Delta Oil...15
Dhaka...23, 24, 25
Dodd, Christopher...28, 108
dredges...45, 46, 47, 48, 54

E
Eagleburger, Lawrence...6
economic growth...23, 96

Economist (magazine)...100, 127, 129

Ecuador...47, 56, 57, 58, 64, 127

Egypt...47, 108, 113, 116

Eizenstat, Stuart...109

El Salvador...65

Electricity...23, 24, 98, 100, 103, 126

Ellicott Business Machine Corporation International...45, 46, 47, 48

embargos - see also sanctions...5, 27, 46, 109

energy...7, 8, 14, 16, 17, 18, 20, 21, 22, 24, 25, 31, 45, 71, 78, 82, 97, 98, 102, 103, 116, 118, 125, 127

Energy, Department of...8, 19

Environmental Protection Agency...8, 91

Estée Lauder...74, 75, 128

European Aeronautic Defense and Space Company (EADS)...53, 54

European Union...9, 34, 59, 60, 61, 62, 63, 108, 113

Evans, Donald...6, 43

exchange rate...32, 102

Export-Import Bank...8, 30, 37, 46, 48, 93, 118, 126, 127

exports...1, 3, 5, 14, 31, 45, 52, 53, 54, 59, 77, 107, 109, 118, 125

F

Farrar, Steve...40

Federal Aviation Administration...91

Finston, Susan Kling...80, 81

Fluor...31

Food and Drug Administration...112

FOPI (*Forum der forschenden pharmazeutischen Industrie*)...63

Ford...35, 45, 48, 49, 50, 51, 76

Ford, Chuck...59

Foreign Affairs (journal)...126, 130

Foreign Assistance Act...86

Foreign Corrupt Practices Act (FCPA)...87

Foreign Relations Committee...28, 108

Foreign Service Act...125, 126

Fox, Vicente...96

France...14, 27, 28, 44, 55, 84, 87, 89, 91, 92, 130

Franco, Itamar...90, 91

Frei, Eduardo...28

G

Gadbaw, Michael...14

Galley, Alexandre...83, 84, 85, 86

Garten, Jeffrey...6, 32, 119, 127, 130

Gbagbo, Laurent...84, 86

General Agreement on Tariffs and Trade (GATT)...69, 71, 79, 86

General Electric...14, 88, 128

General Motors...35

Geneva...9, 69, 81

Georgia...15, 44

Germany...54, 55, 64, 87, 91

Gillespie, Charles A. (Tony)...44, 95

Gillette Company...128

glass...39, 41

globalization...2, 3, 12, 29, 30, 119, 125
Gore, Albert...19, 37, 65
Gore-Chernomyrdin Commission...65
Greenberg, Maurice (Hank)...31
Guardian Industries...39, 40, 41, 42
Guei, Robert...83, 84
Gulf War...55

H
Hagel, Chuck...108
Haiphong...47
Hall, Kathryn...63
Hamilton, Lee...108
Hanoi...46, 47, 48, 50
Hardy, Maura...115
Haripur...23, 25
Harley-Davidson...60, 61
Hat Yai...36
Hauptverband...62
Havana...69, 109
helicopter...94, 95
Helms, Jesse...28, 86, 108, 129
Helms-Burton Act...108
Herzog, Kristine...63, 64
Holzman, John...23, 24
Homeland Security, Department of (DHS)...9, 110, 111, 112, 115, 117
Honda...60, 61
Honduras...112
House International Relations Committee...11, 108
Huntsman, Jon M. Jr....43, 50
Hutchinson, Asa...115
Hyatt Hotels...31

I
Immigration and Naturalization Service...110
imports...1, 3, 5, 34, 39, 40, 41, 49, 97, 110, 118, 125
Inderfurth, Karl F. (Rick)...25
India...56, 65, 81, 82, 97, 98, 99, 100, 101, 108, 109, 110, 119, 127, 129
Indonesia...31, 32, 34, 42, 47, 74, 75, 116, 119, 127
Indo-U.S. High Technology Cooperation Group...82
intellectual property...70, 71, 72, 73, 74, 75, 76, 77, 78, 79, 80, 81, 82, 121, 128
Interior, Department of the...8
International Center for the Settlement of Investment Disputes...70
International Finance Corporation...23
International Intellectual Property Alliance...77, 80, 128
International Maritime Organization...69, 113
International Monetary Fund...2, 34, 35, 58, 69, 126, 130
International Telecommunication Union...70
International Trade Administration...60
International Trade Services Corporation...128
International Wireless...83
investment...1, 2, 4
    foreign direct investment...2, 3, 4, 100

investment bank...14
Iran...2, 15, 107, 108, 110
Iran-Libya Sanctions Act (ILSA)...108, 129
Iraq...2, 110
Israel...65, 82, 108
Italy...127
Itoh, William H. (Will)...32, 33, 34, 35, 37

J
Jacobs, Janice...114
Jakarta...74
Japan...5, 24, 29, 44, 72, 73, 88, 106, 126, 130
Jones, Elizabeth...67
Jordan...47, 82
Juster, Kenneth...82
Justice, Department of...115

K
Kaesshaeffer, John...63, 64
Kansil, Nico...75
Kazakhstan...67, 68, 127
Keita, Ibrahim...83
Kennedy, John F....10
Kerry, John...36
Khon Kaen...36
Khorat...36
Kicker, Scott...25
Kissinger, Henry...36
Klein, Lawrence...125
Kohl, Helmut...55
Kuala Lumpur...30
Kurtzer, Daniel...82
Kuwait Airways...55

L
Labor, Department of...8, 9
Lagos, Ricardo...29
Lane, William...107, 108, 109, 110
Laos...35, 36, 126
Larson, Alan...6, 82
Law of Convertibility...101, 102
Lebanon...2
Levinson, Riva...83
Lewinsky, Monica...109
Libya...2, 108
Lilly...63
Litt, David...18, 19, 22
Lockheed Martin...26, 27
Lord, Winston...47
Lugar, Richard...108

M
M&M chocolate candies — see also chocolate...74, 75

MAGIC (Modern Africa Growth and Investment Company)...83, 85
Mahathir, Mohamad...34
Mahuad, Jamal...57
Malaysia...7, 30, 31, 32, 34, 40, 41, 125, 126
Manzullo, Donald...108
market access...38, 40, 41, 42, 44, 46, 48, 50, 51, 52, 54, 56, 58, 60, 61, 62, 64, 65, 66, 68, 79, 80
Mars Inc....74, 75, 128
Marubeni Corporation...24
Mayr, Alexander...63
McDonald's...2, 31
McDonnell Douglas...26, 53, 54, 55, 56
Meghnaghat...23, 25
Menendez, Robert...99, 100
Mengebier, David...17, 18
Merck...63
Mexico...36, 45, 46, 47, 95, 96, 108, 112, 119, 127
Microsoft...71
Ministry of Foreign Trade and Economic Development (MOFTEC)...73
Miranda, Gilberto...92, 93
Mitterrand, François...55
Morhard, James...11, 12
Morrison, Jim...45, 47
Moscow...65, 66, 67
Motorola...30, 42, 43, 45, 59, 113
Mulroney, Brian...55

N

NAFTA (North American Free Trade Agreement)...46, 89
Nakhon Si Thammarat...36
National Association of Manufacturers...109
National Economic Council...9
National Foreign Trade Council...109
National Oceanic and Atmospheric Administration (NOAA)...91
National Security Council...9, 99
NATO...106, 126
Naval Postgraduate School...90, 128
Netherlands...64
New York Times...2
New Zealand...115, 126
Nguyen Tan Dung...49
Nigeria...65
Nike...31, 77
Niles, Thomas...54, 55
Noboa, Gustavo...57, 59
Nong Khai...36
North Korea...2, 110

O

O'Leary, John...26, 27, 28, 29
Occidental Petroleum...57, 64, 127
Odebrecht...57
Office of Management and Budget...9

oil pipeline...14, 15, 57, 58
Omnibus Trade Act...8
Organization for European Cooperation and Development (OECD)...91, 128
Orr, Robert...30
Overseas Private Investment Corporation (OPIC)...8, 30, 37, 83, 118, 126

P
Pakistan...108, 109, 110
Paraguay...47, 75, 76, 77, 78, 80, 127, 128
Pearson, Robert...10, 15
Peña, Federico...46, 47
Pepper, John...72, 73
Persian Gulf...15, 18, 55
Peterson, Douglas "Pete"...47
Petroecuador...57, 58
Phan Van Khai...47
Pharmaceutical Research and Manufacturers of America (PhRMA)...80, 81, 82
pharmaceuticals...62, 72
Philippine Bureau of Import Services...41
Philippines...31, 32, 34, 41, 126, 127
Pickering, Thomas...65
Pinochet, August...26, 28, 44
Powell, Colin...11
Poza, Carlos...10
Pratt & Whitney...14
Procter & Gamble (P&G)...72, 74, 78
property rights...4, 70, 71, 73, 75, 77, 78, 79, 81, 119, 128
Prueher, Joseph...73
PT Telkom...42, 43

Q/R
Quality Brand Protection Committee (QBPC)...72, 73, 74
Rabat...20
Randt, Clark T. Jr....73
Raytheon...89, 91, 92, 93
Reagan, Ronald...55
regulation...17, 24, 46, 51, 60, 61, 68, 97, 111
Render, Arlene...85, 86
Resolution 1343...84
Richardson, William...19, 24
Rolls-Royce...14
Russia...15, 32, 64, 65, 66, 67, 107, 116

S
sanctions...71, 78, 80, 99, 106, 107, 108, 109, 110, 121, 129
Saudi Arabia...56, 108
Scientific Atlanta...44
security...1, 2, 4, 5, 6, 7, 14, 15, 25, 27, 66, 84, 85, 86, 90, 96, 99, 106, 108, 110, 111, 112, 113, 114, 115, 116, 117, 119, 126, 129, 130
Senate Appropriations Committee...11
SEVIS...129
Shapiro, Charles...26
Sheikh Diab...19

Shultz, George...29
Sikorsky (helicopters)...95
Singapore...22, 23, 30, 31, 126
SIVAM (Amazon Surveillance System)...92, 93, 128
Skol, Michael...87, 88, 93, 94, 95
Slaughter, Matthew...125
Small Business Administration...8
Small Business Exporters Association...45, 47, 109
SOCAR (State Oil Company of the Azerbaijan Republic)...15
software...71, 76, 77, 92, 93, 100, 128
Songkhla...36
South China Sea...29
South Korea...56, 108, 127
Spain...127
Special Consumption Tax...49, 50
State, Department of...5, 6, 8, 9, 10, 19, 30, 46, 52, 88, 93, 99, 111, 113, 114, 115, 117
Strauss, Robert...65
Summers, Lawrence...36
Surabaya...74
Surat Thani...36
Sweden...27, 28, 125
Switzerland...64
Symington-Glenn amendment...109
Syria...2, 110

T
Taiwan...56
Tamil Nadu...97, 98, 99, 100
Taylor, John...99
technology...2, 7, 13, 16, 20, 25, 27, 40, 44, 52, 56, 82, 90, 92, 97, 107, 111, 112, 113, 125, 130
telecommunications...42, 52, 97, 102
Texaco...56, 57, 58
textile...130
Thailand...28, 31, 32, 33, 34, 35, 36, 37, 40, 41, 119, 126, 127
Thatcher, Margaret...55
Thomson-CSF...89
Thurow, Lester...70, 128
Titas Gas Transmission and Distribution Company...23
trade...2, 3, 5, 6, 8, 51
    foreign trade...5
    trade agreements...9, 38, 52, 78, 82, 89, 126, 130
    trade barriers...4, 39, 41, 97
    trade deficit...3
    trade law...69
    trade missions...35, 39, 127
    trade policy...9, 26, 38, 39, 62, 73, 120, 126
    trade preferences...38, 58, 86
Trade Promotion Coordinating Committee...8, 11
Transparency International...67, 88
Transportation, Department of...8, 46
Travel Business Roundtable...117
Treasury, Department of...8, 9, 11, 67, 87, 99, 103, 118

Turkey...15, 32, 81, 127
Twain, Mark...127

U
U.S. Agency for International Development (USAID)...8, 24, 67
U.S. Chamber of Commerce...109, 117
U.S. Commercial Service...5, 8, 46, 50, 53
U.S. Export Assistance Center...46
U.S. Information Agency...8, 24
U.S. Trade and Development Agency (USTDA)...8, 30, 37, 51, 113, 126
U.S. Trade Representative, Office of the (USTR)...5, 9, 40, 43, 50, 65, 79, 80, 81, 118,
    120, 126, 130
U.S.-ASEAN Business Council...30, 31
U.S.-Bangladesh Energy Partnership...25
Udorn...36
United Airlines...31
United Arab Emirates (UAE)...18, 19, 20, 21, 81
United Kingdom...64
Universal Commercial Code...70
Unocal...15, 31
USA PATRIOT Act...129
USA*Engage...107, 108, 109, 110

V
Venezuela...26, 47, 94, 103
Verizon...31
Vietnam...31, 33, 36, 45, 46, 47, 48, 49, 50, 51, 54, 126, 127
    Vietnamese Ministry of Transportation...47
VINAWACO (Vietnam Waterway Construction Corporation)...46, 47
visas...11, 111, 114, 115, 116, 130

W
Wall Street Journal...93, 102, 109, 129
Walters, Paul...30
Wardair...54, 55
Washington consensus...97, 130
Wayne, E. Anthony (Tony)\...114
Western Wireless International...83
Willard, Richard E....128
Williamson, John...130
Wireless Communications Technologies...83
Wittkoff, Peter...90, 92, 128, 129
Wolf, John...6, 7
Woodcock, Kenneth...22, 24
Woolsey, R. James...93, 129
World Bank...2, 23, 34, 69, 86, 88, 99, 103, 109, 126, 130
World Customs Organization...70, 113
World Intellectual Property Organization...69
World Trade Organization...2, 9, 39, 41, 42, 49, 51, 67, 69, 71, 72, 74, 78, 81, 127, 128
World War II...2, 5, 128
Wu Yi...74
Wyeth...63

Y

Yam, John...74
Yeo, Peter...11, 12
Yugoslavia...47

Abbott Laboratories
AES Corporation
Altria Group Inc.
Amerada Hess Corporation
American Council of Engineering Companies
American Express Company
American International Group, Inc.
Anadarko Petroleum Corporation
Ann Ascher, Inc.
Aon Corporation
Aventis
A.T. Kearney, Inc.
Baxter Healthcare Corporation
Bechtel Corporation
The Boeing Company
Booz Allen Hamilton
BP p.l.c.
Bristol-Myers Squibb Company
Burson-Marsteller
Cargill, Inc.
Caterpillar Inc.
Chadbourne & Parke LLP
Chemonics International Inc.
ChevronTexaco Corporation
Chubb Corporation
Citigroup
CMS Energy Corporation
C&O Resources, Inc.
The Coca-Cola Company
ConocoPhillips
Devon Energy Corporation
Duke Energy International
Duncan Macneill Group
Eli Lilly and Company
Eni S.p.A.
EOG Resources, Inc.
Erickson Air-Crane Co.
Ernst & Young International, Ltd.
Estée Lauder Companies
ExxonMobil Corporation
FCA Corp.
FLAG Telecom
Fluor Corporation
Forbes Inc.
Ford Motor Company
General Dynamics
General Electric Company
GlaxoSmithKline p.l.c.
Goldman Sachs & Co.
Guardian Industries Corp.
Halliburton
Holland & Knight LLP
Honeywell International
Ingersoll-Rand Company

International AIDS Vaccine Initiative
Jacobs Engineering
Johnson & Johnson
J.P. Morgan Chase
Kerr-McGee Corporation
Kissinger McLarty Associates
Koch Industries Inc.
Kroll, Inc.
Lazare Kaplan International
Lehman Brothers
Liz Claiborne Inc.
Lockheed Martin
Lova, Inc.
Lucent Technologies
Marathon Oil Corporation
Mars Incorporated
J. Ray McDermott
Medley Global Advisors
Merck & Co., Inc.
Morgan Stanley
Motorola, Inc.
MPRI
Nortel Networks
Northrop Grumman Corporation
Occidental Petroleum Corporation
Old World Industries, Inc.
Oracle Corporation
P&O Nedlloyd Limited
Parsons Brinckerhoff Inc.
The Parsons Corporation
PepsiCo Inc.
Pfizer Inc
Phillips-Van Heusen Corp.
PhRMA
The Port Authority of NY & NJ
Pratt & Whitney Power Systems.
PSEG Global Inc.
QUALCOMM, Inc.
Raytheon Company
Salans
Sara Lee Branded Apparel
Schering-Plough Corporation
Shell International E&P, Inc.
Sikorsky Aircraft Company
TimeWarner Inc.
Turner Construction – International
Tyco Telecommunications
United Parcel Service of America
Unocal Corporation
Vanco Energy Company
Verizon Communications, Inc.
Vintage Petroleum, Inc.
Washington Group International
Wyeth